Ethical & Moral Leadership in Business:

Eliminating Unethical Practices & Building a Culture of Trust & Integrity

Gerard Assey

Ethical & Moral Leadership in Business:
Eliminating Unethical Practices & Building a Culture of Trust & Integrity

By

Gerard Assey

Published by:
Gerard Assey
19/18, Palli Arasan Street
Anna Nagar East
Chennai - 600 102

ISBN: 978-81-985691-8-9

Table of Contents

Disclaimer

All names, characters, organizations, and events depicted in this book are entirely fictitious. Any resemblance to actual persons, living or deceased, or real organizations, is purely coincidental. The case studies and examples provided are intended for illustrative purposes only and are not based on any specific real-life scenarios.

The author has taken care to avoid any references that might be mistakenly interpreted as relating to actual individuals or companies.

This book is intended as a learning resource, and any inferences or interpretations drawn by readers are solely their own.

Preface

Ethics is not just a corporate buzzword; it is the foundation upon which businesses rise or fall. Every decision—whether made in a boardroom, on a factory floor, or in an HR meeting—either strengthens or weakens an organization's ethical core. In today's business world, where trust is currency and integrity is a competitive advantage, ethical leadership is not optional. It is the differentiator between companies that thrive long-term and those that crumble under the weight of scandals and distrust.

This book, '**Ethical & Moral Leadership in Business:** ***Eliminating Unethical Practices & Building a Culture of Trust & Integrity'***, is a guide for leaders, managers, and professionals who recognize that sustainable success is built on ethical decision-making. It is not a theoretical exploration of moral philosophy but a highly practical, real-world playbook designed to help individuals and organizations build cultures of integrity, accountability, and trust.

Why This Book Matters Now More Than Ever

Corporate scandals, fraudulent financial practices, employee mistreatment, and environmental negligence make headlines almost daily. With many companies—once celebrated as industry pioneers—collapsing under the weight of unethical decisions, it's clear that moral shortcuts lead to long-term disasters. Even businesses that survive such crises often face permanent reputational damage, plummeting customer confidence, and legal repercussions that drain their resources.

Yet, ethics in business is not just about avoiding failure. It is about creating an environment where people want to work, where customers trust the brand, and where profits are built on sustainable, ethical foundations. Companies that embrace integrity don't just stay out of trouble—they outperform their competitors. They attract the best talent, earn unwavering customer loyalty, and become trusted brands that stand the test of time.

What This Book Will Teach You

This book is designed as a step-by-step roadmap for identifying ethical challenges, preventing unethical behavior, and fostering an organizational culture that prioritizes moral leadership. It will take you through:

- ✓ The psychological and organizational factors that lead to unethical decisions—and how to counteract them before they escalate.
- ✓ The ripple effect of unethical behavior on employees, communities, and economies.
- ✓ Real-world examples and case studies of companies that collapsed due to ethical failures—and those that turned around by embracing integrity.
- ✓ Proven strategies for developing corporate ethics programs, implementing ethical decision-making models, and creating accountability mechanisms that ensure compliance.
- ✓ How to build a whistleblower protection system that encourages ethical reporting without fear of retaliation.

- ✓ How leaders can inspire ethical behavior at every level and embed integrity into corporate culture.

Who This Book Is For

This book is for business leaders, managers, HR professionals, entrepreneurs, and anyone who believes that ethics should be at the heart of corporate decision-making. Whether you are leading a startup, managing a multinational corporation, or working in a regulatory body, the insights in this book will help you make better, more ethical choices—choices that benefit not just your business, but society as a whole.

A Call to Action

Ethical leadership is not about perfection—it's about commitment. It is about consistently making the right choices, even when they are difficult. It is about creating systems that prevent misconduct rather than just reacting to it. It is about being the kind of leader people trust.

As you embark on this journey through the pages of this book, I encourage you to reflect deeply, challenge existing norms, and take actionable steps to build a workplace where ethics and integrity are non-negotiable. A business that operates ethically is not just good for employees or customers—it is the only way to build a company that stands the test of time.

Let's make ethical leadership the standard, not the exception.

SECTION 1:
THE FOUNDATIONS OF ETHICS IN BUSINESS

Chapter 1: The Importance of Ethics for Organizations

Ethics as the Backbone of Business Success

In the fast-paced and highly competitive corporate world, ethical integrity is often the defining factor between long-term success and eventual downfall. While many organizations chase profits at any cost, history has repeatedly shown that companies built on strong ethical foundations thrive, while those engaged in shady dealings ultimately crumble.

Consider the case of Brightyway Pharmaceuticals, a fictitious but realistic company that started as a small family-owned business manufacturing life-saving drugs. Initially committed to affordability and transparency, Brightyway gained immense trust in the healthcare industry. However, after rapid expansion and leadership changes, unethical cost-cutting measures crept in. The company began underreporting safety risks, manipulating clinical trial data, and charging exorbitant prices for essential medicines.

For a while, profits soared—but then, a scandal broke. Whistleblowers revealed falsified reports, and a lawsuit followed. Within a year, Brightyway's stock plummeted, customer trust eroded, and the company filed for bankruptcy. This story, though fictional, mirrors real-world corporate collapses and underscores one crucial lesson: ethics is not an option—it is a necessity.

Ethics in business isn't just about compliance with laws and regulations; it's about building a culture of trust, responsibility, and sustainability. Companies that uphold ethical standards create environments where employees are proud to work, customers feel valued, and stakeholders remain confident in the organization's integrity.

Why Ethics Matter in Business

At its core, ethics is about doing what is right—even when no one is watching. It dictates how companies interact with customers, treat employees, and impact society. A business without ethics is like a building without a strong foundation—it may stand for a while, but sooner or later, it will collapse.

Imagine two competing companies in the fashion industry: TrooWear Apparel and FlashyTrends Clothing.

TrooWear is committed to fair labor practices, sustainable sourcing, and honest advertising. It ensures that factory workers in developing countries receive fair wages and safe working conditions. On the other hand, FlashyTrends cuts corners, exploits cheap labor, and greenwashes its brand—misleading customers into believing it follows sustainable practices when, in reality, it doesn't.

For a time, both brands grow. However, a major investigative report exposes FlashyTrend's sweatshop conditions and deceptive marketing. Customers boycott the brand, lawsuits emerge, and its reputation is permanently damaged. Meanwhile, TrooWear continues to thrive because consumers value honesty and sustainability.

This example highlights a fundamental truth: Ethical business practices lead to long-term success, while unethical ones are a ticking time bomb.

The Long-Term Benefits of Ethical Conduct

Many companies assume that ethics slow them down or limit their profit potential. The reality, however, is that businesses that prioritize ethics tend to outperform their competitors in the long run. Here's how:

1. Sustainable Growth and Stability

Organizations with strong ethical principles don't have to fear scandals, lawsuits, or regulatory fines. Instead of wasting resources on damage control, they can focus on innovation, expansion, and customer satisfaction.

Consider EverGrow Energy Solutions, a company in the renewable energy sector. From day one, EverGrow was committed to full transparency in its environmental impact, fair wages for workers, and strict adherence to safety regulations. As a result, it gained investor confidence, attracted top talent, and maintained steady growth for over two decades, even when competitors faced regulatory crackdowns.

2. Enhanced Customer Trust and Loyalty

Modern consumers are more informed than ever. They research brands, read reviews, and hold businesses accountable for their actions. When a company upholds ethical values, customers develop trust—and trust leads to long-term loyalty.

Case in Point: EthicalBank is a fictional financial institution that built its brand on honesty and fairness. Unlike traditional banks that rely on hidden fees and predatory lending, EthicalBank ensures total transparency in all transactions. Over time, customers noticed the difference, and even though the bank's fees were slightly higher than competitors, they remained loyal because they valued integrity over short-term savings.

3. Higher Employee Morale and Productivity

Employees want to work for organizations that align with their values. When companies foster a culture of ethics, employees feel respected, valued, and motivated to give their best.

For example, at NovaTechhy Solutions, employees are encouraged to report unethical behavior without fear of retaliation. The company also ensures fair wages, equal opportunities, and clear pathways for growth. As a result, turnover rates are low, employee satisfaction is high, and the company attracts top talent.

4. Competitive Advantage in the Market

Ethical businesses stand out. In an age where corporate scandals frequently make headlines, a company with a spotless reputation has a huge market advantage. Investors are more willing to fund ethical businesses, customers prefer to buy from responsible brands, and regulatory bodies are less likely to impose heavy scrutiny.

How Ethics Impact Brand Reputation, Customer Trust, and Employee Morale

1. Brand Reputation: The Currency of Business

A good reputation takes years to build but only seconds to destroy. Ethical companies cultivate a reputation that attracts loyal customers, investors, and partners.

Take the case of Philharmony Organics, a brand that built its entire identity around ethical farming, fair trade, and eco-friendly packaging. Because of its transparent and honest approach, Philharmony Organics became the go-to choice for health-conscious consumers, even though its products were priced higher than competitors.

In contrast, a fictional company called NutriMaxi marketed itself as a health-conscious brand but was later caught using artificial preservatives and misleading labels. The scandal led to lawsuits, a public backlash, and a drastic drop in sales.

2. Customer Trust: The Key to Longevity

Customers today demand more than just quality products—they want honesty, responsibility, and respect. Companies that uphold ethical values foster strong relationships with their customer base, leading to repeat business and positive word-of-mouth marketing.

Consider the difference between two tech companies offering cloud storage services:

SafeCloudex promises complete privacy and never sells user data to third parties.

DatexVault secretly shares customer information with advertisers.

Once the truth about DatexVault leaks, it loses thousands of customers overnight, while SafeCloudex continues to grow due to its commitment to trust and security.

3. Employee Morale: The Heart of Productivity

Employees who feel their company operates with integrity are more engaged, committed, and productive. Ethical workplaces reduce stress, prevent burnout, and promote a sense of purpose.

At Zen Marketing Solutions, management ensures that promotions are based on merit rather than favoritism. Employees are given a voice, ethical concerns are addressed, and hard work is recognized. This culture leads to high performance, low turnover, and a thriving work environment.

The Role of Corporate Social Responsibility (CSR) in Ethics

Corporate Social Responsibility (CSR) is no longer just a trend—it's an expectation. Companies that actively contribute to society build stronger connections with customers and communities. CSR initiatives can include:

- ✓ Environmental Sustainability: Reducing carbon footprints, promoting recycling, and investing in green technologies.
- ✓ Social Responsibility: Supporting education programs, charity initiatives, and community development projects.
- ✓ Ethical Labor Practices: Ensuring fair wages, safe working conditions, and equal opportunities for all employees.

A great example is EcoffHarvest, a coffee company that sources beans from small farmers at fair prices, reinvests in local communities, and uses sustainable packaging. Customers gladly pay a premium because they know their purchase supports a greater cause.

Ethics is the Future of Business

Ethical businesses don't just survive—they thrive. Organizations that prioritize integrity, transparency, and responsibility not only enjoy long-term financial success but also build strong relationships with customers, employees, and investors.

The choice is simple: A company can either be a Brightyway Pharmaceuticals—rushing toward profits at any cost and facing inevitable collapse—or it can be an EverGrow Energy Solutions—prioritizing ethics and securing a prosperous future.

The question every leader and employee must ask is: ***What kind of organization do we want to build?***

In the next chapter, we will explore the devastating consequences of unethical business practices and how they impact organizations and society.

Chapter 2: The Impact of Unethical Practices on Businesses & Society

The High Cost of Unethical Choices

In the world of business, success is often measured in profit margins, market share, and stock prices. But what happens when a company prioritizes short-term gains over integrity? The answer is simple—destruction.

Unethical business practices may provide a temporary advantage, but they are like termites eating away at the foundation of a building. At first, the structure may appear strong, but over time, the damage becomes irreversible. History is filled with businesses that ignored ethical principles and paid the ultimate price. They lost customers, employees, investors, and, in many cases, their entire existence.

To understand the true cost of unethical practices, let's examine the rise and fall of Tritan Financial Services, a fictitious but very realistic company that went from being a dominant industry player to a cautionary tale in corporate greed.

Case Study: The Rise and Fall of Tritan Financial Services

For nearly two decades, Tritan Financial Services was a respected name in investment banking. Founded by Rick Maslow, a former Wall Street executive, Tritan positioned itself as the go-to firm for high-net-worth individuals and corporate clients looking for innovative financial solutions.

Tritan's success was driven by its promise of delivering exceptional returns on investments. With aggressive marketing and a well-polished image, the firm attracted thousands of clients. At its peak, it managed billions of dollars in assets.

But behind the scenes, a different story was unfolding.

The First Ethical Breach: Misleading Clients

Titan's problems began when the company started overpromising results. Instead of offering realistic projections, Titan's brokers assured clients that their investments were "guaranteed" to grow by at least 20% annually—an impossible promise in the volatile world of finance.

To make matters worse, Tritan fabricated reports to make underperforming investments appear successful. Investors were receiving falsified statements showing consistent growth, even when their actual portfolios were suffering losses.

At first, the deception went unnoticed. The stock market was booming, and Tritan's leadership believed they could "fix" the situation before anyone caught on. But as markets started to slow, the firm began losing money at an alarming rate.

Instead of coming clean, Tritan doubled down on its unethical behavior.

The Second Ethical Breach: Internal Corruption

When lower-level employees discovered the fabricated reports, some raised concerns internally. But instead of addressing the issue, senior executives silenced the whistleblowers. Employees who refused to cooperate were either fired or intimidated into submission.

A culture of fear took over. Employees no longer felt safe speaking up, and ethical decision-making became secondary to protecting the company's reputation at all costs.

The Third Ethical Breach: Fraudulent Accounting

As financial losses mounted, Titan executives began manipulating financial statements to mislead investors and regulatory authorities. Through fraudulent accounting techniques, they made it seem as though the company was still profitable.

Then came the breaking point.

A routine government audit uncovered significant discrepancies in Tritan's records. Investigators found billions of dollars in missing funds, falsified reports, and clear evidence of fraud. The revelations sent shockwaves through the financial world.

The Collapse

Within weeks, Tritan Financial Services declared bankruptcy. Its CEO, Rick Maslow, was arrested for securities fraud. Thousands of investors lost their life savings. Employees were left without jobs.

But the damage didn't stop there. The scandal affected confidence in the entire financial sector. Regulatory agencies tightened their restrictions, other financial firms saw their stocks drop due to declining public trust, and communities that depended on Tritan's investments faced economic downturns.

The fall of Tritan Financial Services serves as a painful reminder: Unethical business practices may provide temporary success, but they always lead to long-term failure.

The Ripple Effect of Unethical Actions

The collapse of a company due to unethical decisions doesn't just affect the business itself. The consequences spread far beyond the boardroom, affecting employees, customers, families, and even entire economies.

Impact on Employees

When a company engages in unethical practices, employees are often the first victims. In Tritan's case, hundreds of employees lost their jobs overnight. Many of them struggled to find new employment because their association with a corrupt company damaged their reputations.

But the damage isn't always financial. Employees who are forced to compromise their ethics often experience stress, anxiety, and emotional exhaustion. A toxic workplace that pressures employees to participate in unethical actions creates a culture of fear and mistrust, leading to low morale and high turnover.

Impact on Customers and Investors

Customers place trust in businesses to deliver fair products and services. When companies engage in fraud or deceptive practices, customer confidence is destroyed. Investors who believed in Tritan's financial reports lost everything, including their retirement savings and college funds for their children.

One investor, a retired school teacher named Lincy Garrett, had invested her life savings with Tritan, trusting the company's promises. When the firm collapsed, she was left with nothing. Stories like hers are common when unethical businesses fail—the people who suffer most are often those who had no control over the wrongdoing.

Impact on the Economy and Society

The collapse of major companies often has wider economic consequences. When a large corporation like Tritan goes bankrupt, it causes:

- ✓ Job losses that ripple through industries and communities.

- ✓ Declines in stock markets as investor confidence drops.
- ✓ Stronger government regulations, leading to increased compliance costs for all businesses.
- ✓ Even honest companies end up paying the price for unethical behavior in their industry because the public loses trust in entire sectors.

How Unethical Decisions Lead to Legal Consequences, Financial Losses, and Public Distrust

Every unethical action has consequences. Some may be immediate, like lawsuits and fines, while others may be long-term, such as loss of reputation and declining customer loyalty.

Legal Consequences

Governments and regulatory agencies have strict laws against fraudulent business practices. Companies caught engaging in unethical behavior face heavy penalties, including:

- ✓ Fines running into millions (or even billions) of dollars.
- ✓ Executives facing prison sentences for fraud, corruption, or embezzlement.
- ✓ Lawsuits from customers, employees, or investors.

When Tritan Financial Services was exposed, Rick Maslow and several executives were sentenced to prison. The company was forced to liquidate all assets to pay back investors—but by then, the damage was irreversible.

Financial Losses

Unethical behavior often leads to short-term financial gains but long-term financial ruin. Companies that

rely on deception eventually lose customers, face legal battles, and suffer revenue losses.
In Tritan's case, once fraud was uncovered, clients pulled their investments, causing the company to spiral into bankruptcy.

Public Distrust

Perhaps the most damaging consequence of unethical practices is loss of trust. Once a company's reputation is destroyed, rebuilding it is nearly impossible. Customers never forget deception.
Would you trust a bank that was once caught stealing customer funds? Would you fly with an airline that was exposed for cutting corners on safety? Trust, once broken, is difficult to restore.

The Unavoidable Truth About Ethics in Business

Every decision a company makes—whether good or bad—has consequences. Ethical businesses build trust, loyalty, and long-term success, while unethical ones may thrive briefly but eventually collapse under the weight of their own wrongdoing.
The story of Tritan Financial Services is not unique. It mirrors real-world cases where businesses that ignored ethics met their downfall.
The lesson here is clear: The cost of unethical behavior is far greater than any short-term profit.
As we move forward in this book, we will explore how businesses can prevent ethical failures, implement strong moral decision-making frameworks, and create workplaces where honesty and integrity are non-negotiable.

Chapter 3: Understanding How Unethical Practices Take Root

The Birth of Unethical Behavior: A Journey into the Human Mind

In the early days of his career, Drey Kelly considered himself an honest man. As a young accountant at Horizon Techmax Solutions, he prided himself on being meticulous, ethical, and fair. He refused to cut corners and believed in transparency. But over time, small pressures, rationalizations, and workplace culture started to chip away at his moral compass.

It started with something small—an adjustment of numbers in financial reports to "align projections" with investor expectations. "Everyone does it," his supervisor assured him. Then came the overstatement of revenue—"It's just to smooth out the numbers for this quarter. We'll correct it in the next one," the CFO told him. Before he knew it, Drey was deep inside a corporate scandal, caught between his initial good intentions and the pressure to conform.

Drey's story is not unique. Across industries, once-ethical individuals find themselves engaging in dishonest practices, often without realizing how far they've strayed. The truth is, unethical behavior rarely begins with a major crime. It begins with small compromises that snowball into larger violations.

The Slippery Slope: How Small Ethical Compromises Lead to Larger Violations

Most people don't wake up one morning and decide to commit fraud. Ethical violations happen gradually, like water wearing away at stone. The journey from honesty to deception is rarely a sudden leap—it's a series of small steps.

Consider Sandra Thomas, a mid-level manager at Vancare Pharmaceuticals. When Sandra first took over the quality control department, she was passionate about ensuring that all medications met safety standards. Then, one day, production was running behind schedule, and a batch of painkillers had a minor defect—nothing dangerous, but slightly below standard.

Her boss told her, "Just approve it, Sandra. If we halt production every time there's a minor issue, we'll never hit our targets."

Sandra hesitated but relented.

The next time, the defect was a little worse. But since she had already compromised once, it was easier to justify doing it again. "It's not a big deal," she told herself. A month later, the company was caught in a full-blown safety scandal, with thousands of patients suffering severe side effects from substandard drugs.

Sandra had never set out to break the law. But her initial small compromise made it easier to make the next one, and before she knew it, she was an accomplice to a crime.

This is the dangerous reality of the slippery slope of unethical behavior—each small compromise makes the next one feel less significant.

Key Psychological Reasons Why People Act Unethically

Unethical behavior isn't always driven by greed or malice. Often, people who engage in dishonest actions are good individuals caught in bad circumstances.

Several psychological factors contribute to ethical decline:

- ✓ Rationalization – "Everyone else is doing it, so it must be okay."
- ✓ Pressure to Perform – Unrealistic sales targets, performance quotas, or financial goals push employees to take shortcuts.
- ✓ Obedience to Authority – Employees may follow unethical orders from superiors, assuming the responsibility isn't theirs.
- ✓ Incremental Changes – Minor ethical compromises create a gradual decline into major violations.
- ✓ Fear of Consequences – Employees may worry that speaking up against wrongdoing could cost them their job or career.

Case Study: The Descent of Next Financial Corporation

At Next Financial Corporation, a leading mortgage lender, the culture of performance pressure overrode ethical considerations.

In the beginning, loan officers were expected to approve only qualified applicants. But over time, leadership pushed for higher numbers. "Get creative," managers told employees. Slowly, employees began approving questionable mortgage applications—first slightly risky ones, then blatantly fraudulent ones.

Within two years, the company was selling massive amounts of high-risk, fraudulent loans to banks. When the housing market crashed, Next collapsed, thousands of people lost their homes, and employees found themselves under federal investigation.

The root cause? The employees did not wake up intending to defraud people. They were drawn in gradually, pressured by unrealistic expectations and an “everyone does it” mentality.

Cultural, Peer, and Systemic Pressures Leading to Moral Compromises

Beyond personal psychology, unethical behavior thrives in environments where cultural, peer, and systemic pressures normalize wrongdoing.

1. The Impact of Workplace Culture

A company’s culture dictates what is acceptable and what isn’t. If a business fosters a culture where success is prioritized over integrity, employees will feel pressure to compromise their ethics.

At Strait Tech, a leading cyber-security firm, new employees were told:

“We don’t ask questions, we just close deals.”

“Results matter more than rules.”

“Winning is everything.”

The company initially thrived with this mindset, but soon, employees began bypassing security protocols, over-promising clients, and manipulating reports. When a major data breach was exposed, customers fled in droves, lawsuits flooded in, and the company shut down.

2. The Role of Peer Influence

People look to their colleagues for guidance on what’s acceptable. If everyone around them is cutting corners, they will feel pressured to do the same.

In one study, employees who worked in teams with high levels of dishonesty were 60% more likely to engage in unethical behavior themselves.

3. Systemic Pressures in Competitive Industries

Certain industries—finance, pharmaceuticals, legal services—are naturally high-pressure. In these environments, employees are often:

- ✓ Told to meet impossible deadlines or targets.
- ✓ Punished for not meeting quotas, even when honesty prevents them from doing so.
- ✓ Encouraged to 'do whatever it takes' to win.

This systemic pressure creates an environment where dishonesty is rewarded, and honesty is punished.

How Minor Policy Violations Escalated into Scandals

Let's examine some realistic fictional scenarios where a single unethical decision spiraled into a full-blown scandal.

Example 1: The Disappearing Safety Reports at Atmost Airlines

At Atmost Airlines, the maintenance team was required to report all aircraft defects before takeoff. Initially, minor issues were logged and repaired.

Then came pressure from management. Delays were costly, and leadership encouraged mechanics to "prioritize important repairs" while ignoring minor ones.

Over time, minor reports stopped being logged. Then, a major mechanical failure caused a crash. Investigations revealed that safety violations had been happening for years, but because it started small, no one had realized how dangerous the situation had become.

Example 2: The Inflated Sales Numbers at Bravish Auto Corp

At Bravish Auto Corp, sales managers were expected to hit high quarterly targets. When sales were slightly behind, managers asked employees to "pre-register" vehicles—counting them as sold before they were actually purchased.

At first, it was just a few cars. Then, to keep up with previous quarters, employees falsified thousands of sales. When the fraud was finally exposed, the company faced government fines, executive resignations, and complete loss of trust in the brand.

Ethical Decision-Making Begins with Awareness

The journey to ethical failure doesn't happen overnight. It begins with small compromises, justified decisions, and pressures that wear people down.

To prevent unethical behavior, organizations must:

- ✓ Encourage transparency and open communication.
- ✓ Set realistic targets that don't force employees into ethical dilemmas.
- ✓ Train employees to recognize early signs of unethical behavior.
- ✓ Create a workplace where speaking up is rewarded, not punished.

Ethics isn't just about avoiding wrongdoing—it's about building a culture where integrity is the foundation of success.

SECTION 2:
THE FRAMEWORK OF ETHICAL & MORAL DECISION MAKING

Chapter 4: Types & Categories of Ethics in Business

When Erene Goodman was appointed as the Chief Ethics Officer at Vancare Medical Systems, she knew she had a challenge ahead of her. The company had been struggling with low employee morale, multiple compliance violations, and growing distrust among patients. Some employees cut corners to meet unrealistic targets, while others turned a blind eye to questionable billing practices. Erene's task was not just about enforcing rules—it was about rebuilding an ethical foundation for the company.

To do that, she first had to understand what kind of ethical dilemmas the organization faced. Were they personal failures of integrity? Professional lapses? Compliance issues? Industry-specific challenges? Or a fundamental flaw in the ethical decision-making framework itself?

This is the challenge many organizations face. What does ethics really mean in a business context? How do different ethical categories shape corporate behavior? And what frameworks guide ethical decision-making?

Understanding the different types and categories of ethics in business is the foundation for creating an ethical workplace. Let's break it down.

Personal Ethics vs. Professional Ethics

Every individual brings personal ethics to the workplace—values and beliefs shaped by upbringing, culture, and personal experiences. However, these personal ethics do not always align with the professional ethics required in a business environment.

The Conflict Between Personal and Professional Ethics

Consider Dan Cambell, a financial advisor at Summit Wealth Solutions. Dan had always believed in honesty and full transparency. But at Summit, hidden fees, misleading sales tactics, and high-pressure selling were common practice.

One day, Dan met Emily Smith, a retired teacher looking to invest her life savings. She trusted Dan to guide her. But company policy encouraged selling high-commission products, even if they weren't the best fit for clients.

Dan had two choices:

Follow his personal ethics and risk losing his job for not pushing company-preferred products.

Adhere to his professional expectations and sell the high-commission product, even though it wasn't in Emily's best interest.

This is a classic example of personal ethics vs. professional ethics conflict—when employees face pressure to compromise their personal integrity for the sake of professional obligations.

Bridging the Gap: Aligning Personal and Professional Ethics

The best companies ensure that professional ethics reinforce personal integrity rather than conflict with it. This means:

- ✓ Establishing clear ethical guidelines that do not force employees into moral dilemmas.
- ✓ Encouraging whistleblowing protections for employees who report unethical practices.

- ✓ Creating a culture where doing the right thing is rewarded, not penalized.

When personal and professional ethics align, employees feel confident making ethical choices, and organizations build long-term trust.

Compliance-Based vs. Value-Based Ethics

Organizations approach ethics in two primary ways:

- ✓ Compliance-Based Ethics – Focused on following rules and regulations to avoid legal trouble.
- ✓ Value-Based Ethics – Rooted in core company values and principles, even beyond legal requirements.

The Pitfalls of Compliance-Based Ethics

At Regular Pharmaceuticals, compliance training was strictly about legal requirements. Employees learned what they could or couldn't do to avoid lawsuits, but ethical decision-making was never discussed.

As a result, when employees found loopholes that were technically legal but ethically questionable, they exploited them. Sales teams misled doctors about drug effectiveness, and production managers pushed unsafe medications because they technically met minimum legal standards.

Eventually, Regular Pharmaceuticals faced a major scandal—not because they broke the law, but because they prioritized compliance over real ethical responsibility.

The Power of Value-Based Ethics

Contrast that with Evergrow Tech Solutions, a company that prioritized integrity over profits. Their ethical policies weren't just about avoiding legal trouble; they were about doing the right thing even when no one was watching.

When a supplier offered cheaper but lower-quality materials, Evergrow's leadership refused—even though it would have saved millions. Their CEO, Mary Lindstrom, said:

"Our values define us, not just the laws we follow. If we build trust, profits will follow."

And she was right. Customers rewarded Evergrow with loyalty, and the company became a leader in ethical business practices.

Why Value-Based Ethics Matter

Companies that go beyond compliance and embed ethical values into their culture build stronger reputations, loyal customers, and high-performing teams. Employees feel proud to work for a company that stands for something greater than profit.

Ethical Challenges in Different Industries

While ethics applies to all businesses, each industry faces unique ethical dilemmas. Let's examine a few examples.

1. Finance: The Temptation of Greed

In the finance industry, ethical lapses often stem from greed and pressure to meet aggressive targets.

At Franklin & Broadway Investment Bank, traders were encouraged to maximize short-term profits at all costs. This led to:

- ✓ Risky, misleading investments that hurt clients.
- ✓ Manipulation of financial reports to hide losses.
- ✓ High-pressure sales tactics that preyed on vulnerable investors.

Ultimately, the bank collapsed during a financial crisis, leaving thousands of customers bankrupt.

Lesson: Financial institutions must prioritize transparency, accountability, and client well-being over short-term profits.

2. Healthcare: The Ethics of Patient Care vs. Profitability

In healthcare, ethical challenges revolve around patient care vs. corporate profit.

At MediCoreFocus Hospitals, doctors were incentivized to perform unnecessary tests and procedures to boost revenue. Patients were subjected to unnecessary surgeries, and insurance companies were billed for treatments that were not medically required.

A whistleblower finally exposed the scheme, and MediCoreFocus faced a billion-dollar lawsuit.

Lesson: Healthcare organizations must prioritize patient well-being over financial incentives.

3. Technology: The Ethics of Data Privacy

Tech companies often grapple with privacy concerns and data security.

At Nimbal AI, a cutting-edge artificial intelligence firm, engineers discovered that their product could predict personal behavior using social media data. Their executives saw an opportunity to sell user data to advertisers—without user consent.

When the public found out, Nimbal AI lost credibility overnight. Users boycotted the company, and regulators fined them millions for privacy violations.

Lesson: Tech companies must balance innovation with ethical responsibility, ensuring user privacy is protected.

Ethical Theories and Frameworks for Decision-Making

Ethical decision-making isn't random—it's guided by philosophical frameworks.

Deontology (Duty-Based Ethics) – Actions are right or wrong based on duty and moral rules.

Example: A journalist refuses to reveal a confidential source, even under legal pressure, because protecting sources is a moral duty.

Utilitarianism (Consequential Ethics) – The best decision is the one that benefits the most people.

Example: A hospital allocates scarce medical resources to maximize lives saved.

Virtue Ethics (Character-Based Ethics) – Decisions should reflect good character traits like honesty and compassion.

Example: A CEO refuses to lay off employees despite financial struggles because loyalty and fairness matter.

Each of these frameworks offers a different perspective on ethical dilemmas, helping organizations and leaders navigate tough decisions.

Ethics as the Foundation of Long-Term Success

Companies that prioritize ethics are not just legally compliant—they are resilient, reputable, and respected.

By understanding the different types of ethics, aligning personal and professional values, fostering a value-driven culture, and applying ethical decision-making frameworks, businesses can prevent scandals, build trust, and create lasting success.

The question every leader and employee must ask is:

Are we just following rules, or are we truly committed to doing what's right?

This commitment to ethics is what separates companies that endure from those that crumble under the weight of their moral failures.

Chapter 5: The Process of Ethical Decision-Making

Ethics in the Real World

When Nina Patwick, the newly appointed Operations Manager at Branlon Tech, received an email from her CEO, she felt a knot in her stomach. The message instructed her to overlook certain product defects in the company's latest line of home security devices. The CEO reasoned that the chances of failure were minimal, and rushing to market would outpace competitors.

Nina had spent years building her reputation as an honest professional. But now, she faced a dilemma: Should she follow orders and risk customer safety? Or should she push back and potentially jeopardize her job?

Ethical decisions like these happen every day in businesses around the world. Some dilemmas are small—like whether to expense a personal meal to the company—while others have life-changing consequences.

Making the right ethical decision requires a structured process. Without it, individuals and businesses risk making choices based on fear, pressure, or short-term gain—all of which can lead to disastrous outcomes.

In this chapter, we will explore a six-step ethical decision-making model that provides a clear roadmap for navigating ethical challenges.

The 6-Step Ethical Decision-Making Model

Many ethical failures don't happen overnight. They occur when small compromises go unchecked. A structured process ensures that decisions are thoughtful, responsible, and sustainable.

Step 1: Identify the Ethical Issue

Every ethical decision begins with recognizing that a dilemma exists. The challenge is that unethical choices often disguise themselves as "business decisions."

For example, at Lamsen Pharmaceuticals, a research team discovered that a popular painkiller had potential long-term side effects. The legal team insisted that there was no legal obligation to disclose this immediately, but some scientists felt an ethical duty to inform the public.

This scenario poses an ethical question: Should the company proactively warn consumers or wait until forced to do so?

To identify an ethical issue, ask:

- ✓ Does this decision align with our values and mission?
- ✓ Could this harm customers, employees, or stakeholders?
- ✓ Would I be comfortable if this decision were made public?

Once an issue is recognized as an ethical concern, it must be addressed rather than ignored.

Step 2: Gather Relevant Information

Informed decisions require accurate data. Without facts, context, and different perspectives, ethical choices may be based on assumptions rather than reality.

When Elliot Ramson, the HR Director of Summat Retailing, discovered that female employees were consistently paid less than their male counterparts, he wanted to take action. But before confronting leadership, he needed solid data.

So, he:

- ✓ Reviewed salary records for the past five years.
- ✓ Interviewed employees to understand their experiences.
- ✓ Studied legal frameworks on pay discrimination.

Armed with facts, Elliot presented an undeniable case to leadership, leading to policy reforms.

The lesson? Ethical decisions must be rooted in evidence, not emotion.

Step 3: Evaluate Options Using Ethical Frameworks

Once the facts are clear, the next step is to evaluate possible courses of action using ethical principles.

Let's revisit Nina Patwick's dilemma at Branlon Tech. She had two options:

- ✓ Approve the defective product, risking customer safety but ensuring a competitive market advantage.
- ✓ Reject the product launch, prioritizing safety but delaying profits.

Using ethical frameworks, Nina analyzed her options:

- ✓ Deontology (Duty-Based Ethics): "I have a duty to protect customers, even if it costs the company."
- ✓ Utilitarianism (Greatest Good for the Greatest Number): "If we release a defective product,

customers will suffer, leading to lawsuits and loss of trust."

- ✓ Virtue Ethics (Character and Integrity): "What kind of leader do I want to be? Can I live with this decision?"

By evaluating her options through different lenses, Nina saw that compromising on safety was not an option.

When making ethical decisions, leaders must consider not just legality but morality.

Step 4: Consider Stakeholders and Potential Consequences

Ethical decisions rarely affect just one person—they have a ripple effect across employees, customers, investors, and the community.

When Jerome Varky, CEO of LightSolar Energy, discovered that a supplier was using child labor in its factories, he had to decide:

Cut ties immediately, which would delay LightSolar's major project and cost millions.

Negotiate reforms, pressuring the supplier to change its labor practices over time.

To weigh his options, Jerome mapped out who would be affected by each choice:

If he cut ties: The project would be delayed, investors might panic, but LightSolar would maintain its ethical standards.

If he stayed with the supplier: The project would continue smoothly, but LightSolar would be complicit in exploiting children.

After consulting human rights experts and his leadership team, Jerome terminated the contract, choosing long-term integrity over short-term convenience.

Stakeholder analysis ensures that decisions do not prioritize profits at the expense of people.

Step 5: Make a Decision and Take Action

The hardest part of ethical decision-making is having the courage to act. Many people know the right thing to do but fear consequences.

At Regal HealthSolutions, when whistleblower Samantha Leigh exposed that doctors were falsifying patient records to inflate insurance claims, she risked everything—her job, her reputation, and potential legal battles.

But Samantha knew that staying silent was not an option. She:

- ✓ Documented all evidence to support her claims.
- ✓ Consulted legal experts to understand her protections.
- ✓ Reported the fraud to internal compliance officers and, when ignored, to regulators.

Her bravery led to massive reforms in the company and saved patients from medical fraud.

Making ethical choices requires conviction, preparation, and action—even in the face of adversity.

Step 6: Reflect and Improve Future Decision-Making

Every ethical decision offers lessons for the future. Organizations that learn from past ethical dilemmas become stronger, more resilient, and more trustworthy.

After a major public relations crisis over environmental violations, Evergreen Products implemented a mandatory ethics review for all major decisions. They also:

- ✓ Created a whistleblower protection program.
- ✓ Conducted ethics training for all employees.
- ✓ Set up an independent ethics board to review policies.

The result? Evergreen transformed its reputation, proving that businesses can recover from ethical missteps through accountability and improvement.

Every ethical decision—good or bad—should lead to reflection, policy refinement, and stronger safeguards.

Final Thoughts: Ethics as a Competitive Advantage

Ethical decision-making is not just about avoiding scandals. It's about building a foundation of trust, sustainability, and long-term success.

Companies like Evergreen Products, LightSolar Energy, and Summat Retailing thrive because they understand:

Ethical businesses do not just survive. They lead.

The question is: When faced with an ethical dilemma, will you have the courage to choose what's right?

A company's true character is revealed not in easy moments, but in difficult ones. And the organizations that prioritize ethics today will be the industry leaders of tomorrow.

Chapter 6: Identifying Ethical Weaknesses in Your Organization

The Hidden Cracks in a Business's Moral Foundation

On the surface, FerroGoods Industries appeared to be an ethical and thriving company. Their mission statement spoke of integrity, trust, and commitment to social responsibility. They had glossy brochures detailing employee well-being initiatives and a corporate social responsibility (CSR) program that contributed to local charities.

But underneath this polished exterior, the reality was different. Employees whispered about managers who silenced dissenting voices. Promotions were based on favoritism, not merit. The sales team, under pressure to meet aggressive targets, inflated revenue numbers and over-promised to clients.

When FerroGoods was hit with a major lawsuit after a whistleblower exposed fraudulent practices, leadership scrambled to defend itself. They claimed ignorance, but the truth was that the warning signs had been there for years—they had just chosen to ignore them.

Most organizations do not start out unethical. Unethical behavior takes root gradually, often in the form of small compromises, overlooked behaviors, and a lack of accountability. This is why businesses must be proactive in identifying ethical weaknesses before they spiral into crises.

This chapter will help you assess whether your organization has hidden ethical flaws and provide a structured approach to recognizing and fixing them.

How to Detect an Unethical Work Culture

A company's culture is not defined by its slogans or values displayed on walls—it is shaped by the everyday behaviors, decisions, and interactions of its people. When an organization begins to drift into unethical territory, there are always warning signs. The problem is, many businesses ignore them until it's too late.

Case Study: The Culture Shift at Greystone Financials

Greystone Financials was once a company known for ethical leadership. But when a new CEO took over, profitability became the sole focus. Employees noticed subtle changes:

- ✓ Sales representatives were pressured to push risky investments onto clients.
- ✓ Internal audits were delayed to avoid uncovering compliance violations.
- ✓ Managers discouraged employees from raising ethical concerns, labeling them as "not team players."

Within three years, Greystone Financials had lost the trust of its employees and clients, resulting in regulatory fines and plummeting stock prices.

Lesson: Ethical decline never happens overnight—it is a slow process that begins when companies start prioritizing short-term gains over long-term integrity.

Red Flags That Indicate Ethical Weaknesses

If your organization exhibits any of these signs, it may have ethical vulnerabilities:

- ✓ Lack of Transparency: Leaders withhold information, manipulate numbers, or operate behind closed doors.
- ✓ Tolerance for Small Misconducts: Brushing off small ethical violations (e.g., falsifying minor expenses) sets the stage for bigger fraud.
- ✓ Fear-Based Culture: Employees hesitate to report unethical behavior due to fear of retaliation.
- ✓ Conflicts of Interest: Leaders and managers make decisions that personally benefit them, rather than the company.
- ✓ Unrealistic Performance Goals: When targets are too aggressive, employees feel pressured to cut ethical corners to meet them.
- ✓ Frequent Turnover in Key Roles: Ethical workplaces attract and retain talent, while unethical ones see high turnover, particularly among employees with strong values.
- ✓ Leadership Hypocrisy: If top executives preach ethics but act differently, employees follow their behavior, not their words.

Recognizing these signs is the first step. The next step is conducting a thorough ethical self-assessment.

Conducting an Ethical Self-Assessment & Audit

Businesses regularly assess financial health, operational efficiency, and customer satisfaction, but few take the time to audit their ethical climate.

An Ethical Self-Assessment is a structured process that helps organizations uncover weaknesses, blind spots, and potential risks.

Steps to Conduct an Ethical Audit

Step 1: Gather Anonymous Employee Feedback

The most honest insight about workplace ethics comes from employees on the ground. However, many hesitate to speak up if they fear retaliation.

To get genuine feedback:

- ✓ Create anonymous surveys that allow employees to report ethical concerns without fear.
- ✓ Hold confidential one-on-one interviews with employees across departments.
- ✓ Encourage open discussion forums where employees can share observations.

Example: When Klenman Logistics noticed a sharp decline in employee engagement, they conducted an anonymous ethics survey. The results revealed widespread complaints of managers coercing employees to work unpaid overtime. Leadership took corrective action and introduced strict labor compliance policies.

Step 2: Examine Policies & Practices

Having a Code of Ethics is meaningless if it is not practiced. Companies must regularly assess:

- ✓ Whether policies on ethics and compliance are enforced.
- ✓ If there are clear reporting mechanisms for unethical behavior.
- ✓ Whether employees feel protected when raising concerns.

Example: BrightLight Retail had a whistleblower policy on paper, but when an employee reported a case of internal fraud, management dismissed it. The company realized their policy was ineffective and created an independent ethics committee to handle complaints.

Step 3: Evaluate Leadership Behavior

An organization's ethical climate is set by its leaders. Employees watch what leaders do—not just what they say.

To assess leadership ethics:

- ✓ Monitor whether executives follow the same rules they set for others.
- ✓ Observe how leaders handle ethical dilemmas.
- ✓ Check if managers reward integrity or only prioritize results.

When leaders act ethically, it trickles down into the entire organization.

Recognizing Red Flags in Policies, Leadership, and Employee Conduct

Policies That Encourage Unethical Behavior

- ✓ Sales commissions without ethics guidelines (leading to false promises to customers).
- ✓ Lenient penalties for ethical violations, which make misconduct seem acceptable.
- ✓ Lack of diversity and inclusion policies, which can lead to discrimination.

Leadership Red Flags

- ✓ Senior management ignores concerns or retaliates against whistleblowers.
- ✓ Company leaders make questionable financial decisions that personally benefit them.
- ✓ Executives have a "results-at-any-cost" mindset, pressuring employees to compromise ethics.

Employee Conduct Warning Signs

- ✓ Employees frequently bend rules to meet goals.

- ✓ Fear of reporting unethical behavior due to lack of trust in leadership.
- ✓ High turnover of employees who value ethics, leaving behind only those who comply with a toxic culture.

When these issues go unchecked, they lead to scandals, lawsuits, and reputational damage.

Creating an Ethics Scorecard for Internal Evaluation

To ensure continuous ethical improvement, companies should measure their progress with an Ethics Scorecard.

How to Build an Ethics Scorecard

Example: NovyTech Solutions implemented a quarterly Ethics Scorecard and found that many employees felt uncomfortable reporting unethical behavior. In response, they strengthened their whistleblower protections and trained managers on ethical leadership.

Final Thoughts: Strengthening the Ethical Core of Your Business

Ethical weaknesses do not make a company bad—they make it human. The difference between successful, long-lasting organizations and those that collapse lies in their willingness to recognize and correct these weaknesses.

The strongest businesses are not the ones that never make mistakes—they are the ones that actively look for weaknesses and fix them before they turn into disasters.

The question is: *Will your company be proactive in addressing ethical weaknesses, or will it wait until a crisis forces change?*

SECTION 3:
BUILDING AN ETHICAL ORGANIZATION

Chapter 7: Strategies for Preventing Unethical Practices

The Foundation of an Ethical Organization

Imagine stepping into the headquarters of LanternTech Solutions, a fast-growing software company. The walls of the office are adorned with posters that say, “Integrity Above All”, and the company handbook clearly outlines a zero-tolerance policy for unethical behavior. Yet, behind the scenes, things look very different.

Employees regularly manipulate project timelines to meet unrealistic deadlines. Sales teams overpromise features that don’t exist yet, and managers turn a blind eye to questionable hiring practices to bring in "top talent." Despite its official stance on ethics, LanternTech’s culture breeds dishonesty.

Not surprisingly, within a few years, the company faced multiple lawsuits, lost key clients, and struggled with high employee turnover. It wasn’t that the leadership intended for unethical practices to thrive—it happened because they failed to build a system that actively prevented and discouraged misconduct.

The lesson here is simple: a company’s ethical foundation is not built on words, but on actions, systems, and accountability.

Many organizations believe they are ethical because they have a code of conduct or an HR policy that outlines appropriate behavior. But these are merely documents—true ethical integrity is woven into the company's everyday decisions, policies, leadership behaviors, and accountability measures.

To prevent unethical practices from taking root, businesses must intentionally design an environment where ethical behavior is not only encouraged but expected, rewarded, and enforced.

This chapter provides a detailed roadmap on how organizations can build strong ethical defenses, focusing on:

- ✓ Designing policies that reinforce ethical behavior
- ✓ Implementing clear codes of conduct and ethics training
- ✓ Holding leaders and employees accountable
- ✓ Rewarding ethical behavior and discouraging misconduct

By the end of this chapter, you will have a clear, actionable plan to strengthen the ethical foundation of your business—before unethical practices take root.

Step 1: Designing Policies That Reinforce Ethical Behavior

A policy is only as good as its enforcement. Many businesses have beautifully crafted ethics policies that no one follows because they are either too vague, unenforced, or irrelevant to daily work.

An ethical policy must be:

- ✓ Clear and specific—Employees must understand exactly what is expected.
- ✓ Actionable—It must outline what happens when ethical violations occur.
- ✓ Integrated into everyday work—It should not be a one-time document but part of decision-making processes.

Case Study: The Transformation of Arnold Pharmaceuticals

Arnold Pharmaceuticals had a problem: sales teams routinely exaggerated the effectiveness of drugs to doctors and hospitals to increase sales. When a regulatory body launched an investigation, the company faced a serious reputation crisis.

Instead of simply issuing a public apology, the company took aggressive action:

They rewrote their sales policies, explicitly banning misrepresentation of product efficacy.

They implemented real-time monitoring, where sales pitches were randomly audited.

Bonuses were restructured to focus on customer satisfaction rather than pure sales numbers.

The result? In three years, complaints dropped by 90%, and Arnold became a case study in turning around an unethical corporate culture.

How to Create Policies That Work

To ensure ethical policies are not just words on paper, businesses must:

- ✓ Review existing policies and identify loopholes that could enable unethical behavior.
- ✓ Consult employees—they often see ethical challenges that leadership overlooks.
- ✓ Integrate policies into daily decisions, ensuring managers and employees use them actively.
- ✓ Ensure consistency—ethical standards must apply to everyone, from interns to CEOs.

Without strong policies that are actively implemented, ethical behavior remains a suggestion, not an expectation.

Step 2: Implementing Clear Codes of Conduct and Ethics Training

A Code of Conduct should not be a long, unreadable document—it should be a living, breathing guide that is practical, relatable, and actively used in the organization.

A well-designed Code of Conduct should:

- ✓ Be short and simple—people won't follow something they don't understand.
- ✓ Use real-world examples of ethical dilemmas employees might face.
- ✓ Be reinforced through training and daily decision-making.

Why Ethics Training Often Fails

Most companies conduct one-time ethics training that is boring, theoretical, and disconnected from real challenges. Employees attend because they have to, but they don't absorb the content.

Solution? Make it practical and ongoing.

Use real-life case studies from within the company (while keeping them anonymous).

Create interactive sessions where employees discuss ethical dilemmas they have faced.

Train leaders first—they must model ethical behavior for employees to follow.

Example: At Horizon Group, instead of PowerPoint-driven ethics training, employees were given realistic ethical dilemmas in workshops, such as:

"A supplier offers you a personal gift in exchange for a contract—what do you do?"

"A customer asks for a small favor that goes against company policy. How do you handle it?"

Employees engaged more actively, and ethical awareness increased significantly across the company.

Step 3: Holding Leaders and Employees Accountable

Many businesses fail ethically not because of bad policies but because of selective enforcement.

When top executives or high-performing employees get away with misconduct, it sends a message that ethics are optional.

Case Study: The Downfall of Redneck Financial Services

At Redneck Financial Services, junior employees were regularly fired for minor compliance violations, but senior executives were protected despite engaging in insider trading. Eventually, a whistleblower exposed the corruption, leading to a criminal investigation, lawsuits, and a complete collapse of the firm.

Lesson: Ethics must apply equally to everyone, or they will not apply at all.

Building an Accountability System

- ✓ Establish confidential reporting channels where employees can report misconduct without fear.
- ✓ Create an independent ethics committee that investigates violations fairly.
- ✓ Take immediate action when violations occur, regardless of the employee's rank.

When accountability is real and visible, ethical behavior becomes a genuine expectation.

Step 4: Rewarding Ethical Behavior and Discouraging Misconduct

Most companies only punish ethical violations—they forget to reward ethical behavior. But if ethical choices are never acknowledged or incentivized, employees may feel there's no real benefit in doing the right thing.

How to Reward Ethical Behavior

- ✓ Integrate ethics into performance reviews—Employees should be evaluated not just on results but on how they achieve them.
- ✓ Publicly recognize employees who demonstrate integrity, even in difficult situations.
- ✓ Ensure ethical leadership is part of promotion criteria—managers should be selected not just for results but for ethical behavior.

Example: At Hamrock Consulting, the company introduced an Integrity Award, where employees could nominate peers who demonstrated exceptional ethical behavior. Within a year, reports of ethical violations decreased, and employees began taking greater pride in their ethical choices.

Final Thoughts: Ethics as a Competitive Advantage

Preventing unethical practices is not just about avoiding scandals—it is about building an organization that people trust, respect, and want to be a part of.

An ethical company:

- ✓ Attracts top talent—people want to work where integrity is valued.
- ✓ Earns customer loyalty—trust is the foundation of lasting business relationships.
- ✓ Avoids costly scandals—ethical companies rarely face lawsuits and reputational damage.

Ultimately, the choice is simple: Build ethics into your company now, or pay the price later.

Chapter 8: The Role of Leadership in Setting Ethical Standards

The True Power of Leadership in Shaping Ethics

Imagine two companies—Venture Group and Bramton Incorporated—both operating in the same industry, offering similar services, and competing for the same market share.

At Venture Group, employees feel empowered to speak up when they notice something wrong. Their CEO, Ezekiel Carter, has built a culture where honesty and transparency are rewarded, and wrongdoing is not tolerated, no matter who commits it.

At Bramton Incorporated, things are different. Employees hesitate to report issues because managers protect high-performers, even if they act unethically. The leadership team preaches ethics but practices favoritism, making it clear that success matters more than integrity. Over time, small ethical compromises snowball into widespread corruption, financial manipulation, and legal troubles.

What made the difference?

It wasn't policy manuals or HR training sessions. It was leadership.

A company's ethical foundation is not built in boardrooms or legal documents—it is built in the daily actions of its leaders. Employees watch their leaders closely. If executives cut corners, manipulate numbers, or bend rules, employees take that as permission to do the same.

Conversely, when leaders set a high ethical bar and enforce it consistently, employees follow suit. The tone at the top sets the tone for the entire organization.

In this chapter, we will explore how ethical leadership defines corporate culture, the importance of leading by example, a real-world-inspired case study of an ethical transformation, and the key traits of ethical leaders that every organization needs.

Ethical Leadership and Corporate Culture: A Mirror Effect

Corporate culture is like a mirror—it reflects the values, behaviors, and priorities of leadership. The question is: What kind of reflection is your leadership creating?

If leaders are honest, fair, and accountable, employees will mirror those behaviors. If leaders bend the rules, prioritize profits over principles, or tolerate dishonesty, employees will follow suit.

Consider the case of Oliver Johnson, CEO of Merrick Financial Solutions. When he took over the struggling firm, he found a culture of unethical sales practices, where employees pressured clients into risky investments and hid potential losses. Instead of blaming employees, he examined the leadership structure.

What he found was shocking:

Sales managers were rewarding unethical behavior—employees who manipulated numbers got bonuses, while those who followed ethical guidelines were underpaid.

Senior executives ignored complaints—whistleblowers were dismissed as “troublemakers.”

There was no accountability—leaders who broke rules faced no consequences.

Jensen realized that to fix the company, he had to fix the leadership first.

He fired senior leaders who encouraged unethical behavior, restructured incentives to reward ethical performance, and set strict penalties for dishonesty.

Within two years, Merrick Financial Solutions transformed from a scandal-ridden firm to an industry leader in ethical financial advising.

The lesson? Unethical culture is never a grassroots problem—it is a leadership problem. Fix the leadership, and the culture will follow.

The Power of Leading by Example

Every leader must ask themselves: Would I want my employees to act the way I do?

A leader who preaches honesty but fudges numbers, or talks about integrity but takes shortcuts, creates a culture of hypocrisy. Employees notice inconsistencies and act accordingly.

The most effective ethical leaders don't just talk about values; they demonstrate them through actions.

Take the example of Sophia Mackey, the COO of NoahTech Innovations. One day, a major client offered her a $1 million under-the-table deal to prioritize their contract over competitors. Legally, no one would have found out. It was an easy way to secure a massive bonus.

Instead of accepting, she immediately reported the bribe to her board. She also held a company-wide town hall, sharing the story (without revealing client details) and reinforcing why NoahTech never compromises ethics for profits.

What was the result?

- ✓ Employees realized ethical behavior was non-negotiable.
- ✓ Trust in leadership skyrocketed—people saw she practiced what she preached.
- ✓ NoahTech's reputation grew, attracting clients who valued integrity.

One leader's single decision sent a powerful message across the company.

Ethical leadership is about demonstrating the right behavior, even when no one is watching. When leaders lead by example, ethical decision-making becomes the norm, not the exception.

Case Study: Turning Around an Unethical Organization

The Fall and Rise of Callen Industries

Callen Industries, a global manufacturing giant, was once known for bribing officials, falsifying safety reports, and exploiting workers. When the company's new CEO, Mark Raymonds, took over, he found a culture built on deception and fear. Employees didn't trust management, and unethical behavior was deeply ingrained.

Instead of quick fixes, Raymonds implemented a three-step transformation plan:

Zero-Tolerance Leadership

- ✓ He fired executives who engaged in unethical practices.
- ✓ He implemented strict consequences for dishonesty, regardless of seniority.

Transparency and Open Communication

- ✓ Employees could anonymously report ethical concerns.

- ✓ He held monthly Q&A sessions, openly discussing ethical challenges.

Ethics as a Competitive Advantage

- ✓ He made ethics a selling point in marketing campaigns.
- ✓ Clients began choosing Calden for its commitment to responsible business.

Within three years, Callen Industries went from scandal-ridden to an industry benchmark in ethical manufacturing. Profits grew, employee satisfaction soared, and the company regained its reputation.

The turnaround happened not because of new policies, but because of ethical leadership at the top.

The Core Traits of Ethical Leaders

All ethical leaders share certain traits that influence their decision-making and leadership style. These qualities define how they navigate moral dilemmas and inspire trust.

1. Integrity

Ethical leaders do what is right, even when it's inconvenient. They never let profit override principles.

2. Accountability

They hold themselves and others responsible. They don't blame others for failures but take ownership of problems.

3. Transparency

They communicate openly, even when the truth is difficult to hear. Employees trust leaders who don't hide bad news.

4. Courage

It takes boldness to resist unethical pressure. Ethical leaders have the courage to say no, even when others cave in.

5. Empathy

They care about the impact of their decisions on employees, customers, and society. Ethical leaders value people over profits.

Final Thoughts: Why Ethical Leadership is the Future

In today's world, ethical leadership is not optional—it's a competitive advantage. Companies that build a culture of trust, honesty, and accountability don't just avoid scandals—they attract the best talent, earn customer loyalty, and build sustainable success.

A leader's personal commitment to integrity can determine whether an organization thrives ethically or collapses in corruption. The question is:

What kind of leader will you be?

Will you set a high ethical standard that others follow, or will you allow shortcuts and compromises to define your leadership?

The choice is yours—but the consequences will shape your organization for years to come.

Chapter 9: Handling Ethical Issues & Whistleblowing Cautions

The Challenge of Speaking Up in an Unethical Environment

In the offices of YouAreWell Pharmaceuticals, employees once spoke in hushed tones about an open secret. Sales executives had been manipulating drug trial results to make their medications look more effective than they actually were. Everyone knew it was happening, yet no one dared to speak up.

Lisa Cotter, a mid-level research analyst, saw the problem firsthand. The data didn't add up, but when she raised concerns with her immediate supervisor, he brushed it off.

"Don't worry about it, Lisa. This is how the industry works. Besides, do you want to risk your job over something no one else seems to mind?"

Lisa faced a difficult choice. If she ignored the issue, she would be complicit in a deception that could harm patients worldwide. If she spoke up, she risked losing her job, alienating colleagues, and facing legal battles.

This is the reality of ethical dilemmas in the workplace. Many employees want to do the right thing, but the fear of retaliation, job loss, or isolation keeps them silent. Organizations must build a culture where ethical concerns are addressed without fear, and where employees who speak up are protected, not punished.

The Role of Ethics Committees and Compliance Teams

Companies that take ethics seriously do not leave ethical decision-making to chance. They create structured mechanisms to handle ethical concerns effectively. Two essential components of this framework are ethics committees and compliance teams.

At Ranguard Tech Solutions, the leadership team understood the importance of proactively managing ethics rather than reacting to scandals. They established an independent ethics committee, separate from the executive board, with three key responsibilities:

- ✓ Investigating ethical concerns raised by employees
- ✓ Recommending disciplinary actions for ethical violations
- ✓ Ensuring company policies align with ethical best practices

Meanwhile, their compliance team worked on the technical side of ethics, ensuring the company followed regulatory laws, anti-bribery policies, and corporate governance rules.

One year after implementing these structures, Ranguard Tech saw a 40% increase in employees reporting ethical concerns—not because the company had more problems, but because employees finally felt safe speaking up.

A well-functioning ethics committee can make the difference between a company that addresses issues internally and one that makes headlines for all the wrong reasons.

Building an Effective Whistleblower Protection Program

Most companies claim they support whistleblowers, but when push comes to shove, many fail to protect them. Employees need assurance that they won't face retaliation for reporting misconduct.

So, how do organizations build a system that genuinely protects and encourages ethical reporting?

1. Anonymity and Confidentiality

A whistleblower program must allow employees to report concerns without fear of exposure. This can be done through:

Anonymous hotlines managed by external firms

Secure internal reporting systems that do not track employees' identities

Legal protections that prevent companies from retaliating against whistleblowers

2. Clear and Accessible Reporting Channels

At Ellen Financial Services, whistleblower complaints could be submitted via a 24/7 hotline, a dedicated email, or a mobile app. Employees had multiple options to ensure ease of access.

3. Non-Retaliation Policies with Strong Enforcement

Whistleblower programs mean nothing if employees fear retaliation. Organizations must create policies that explicitly prohibit retaliation and ensure that violators—especially managers—face serious consequences.

4. Leadership Commitment to Ethics

When top executives actively endorse and use the whistleblower program, employees trust it more. A culture of openness starts at the top.

The Risks and Benefits of Whistleblowing

The truth is, whistleblowing is not easy. It can be professionally and emotionally exhausting, leading to:

- ✓ Job loss or demotion
- ✓ Legal battles
- ✓ Industry blacklisting
- ✓ Emotional stress and anxiety

Yet, whistleblowing has also led to some of the most important corporate accountability moments in history. Consider the case of Nathan Dawson, a compliance officer at Strategic Energy Corp.

Nathan discovered that his company was illegally dumping toxic waste into nearby rivers. He reported it to his supervisors, who dismissed his concerns. Realizing the gravity of the situation, he filed an official complaint with the regulatory authorities.

The fallout was swift. Strategic Energy paid a $500 million fine, its CEO resigned, and stricter environmental policies were put in place. Nathan, however, lost his job and struggled to find work in the industry.

But years later, he became a leading advocate for corporate environmental responsibility and was awarded for his efforts in exposing corporate malpractice.

Whistleblowing is often a personal and professional sacrifice, but it can lead to real change.

Organizations that value ethics must not just tolerate whistleblowers but protect, support, and reward them.

Case Study: The Whistleblower Who Changed an Industry

Edna Marshal: The Accountant Who Took Down a Billion-Dollar Fraud

Edna Marshal was a senior accountant at Lanning Group, a multinational conglomerate. Over time, she noticed serious financial discrepancies in the company's statements. Profits were being inflated, losses were hidden, and shareholders were being misled.

When she confronted her CFO, he told her, *"That's how we do things here. It's harmless."*

Edna had a choice: stay silent and protect her career or expose the fraud. She chose the latter.

She first reported her concerns internally, but they were ignored. She then went to government regulators, providing detailed financial evidence of misconduct.

The impact was seismic:

Lanning Group collapsed, leading to one of the biggest corporate fraud cases in history.

The CEO, CFO, and multiple executives were arrested.

New laws were enacted to prevent similar fraud in the future.

However, Edna paid a personal price. She faced industry blacklisting, legal threats, and media scrutiny. But she also became a symbol of courage and integrity, proving that one person's decision to speak up can change an entire industry.

Her story serves as a powerful reminder: Ethical decision-making is never easy, but it is necessary.

Final Thoughts: Creating a Culture That Supports Ethical Reporting

Organizations that truly value ethics must go beyond just having policies on paper. They must:

- ✓ Create independent ethics committees to oversee ethical concerns.
- ✓ Ensure whistleblower programs are secure, anonymous, and accessible.
- ✓ Enforce strict non-retaliation policies to protect employees.
- ✓ Train leaders to support and respond to ethical concerns appropriately.

Most importantly, leaders must ask themselves:

"Are we building a culture where employees feel safe speaking up, or one where silence is the only option?"

When ethical reporting is encouraged, supported, and protected, businesses thrive—not just in reputation, but in long-term sustainability. The future belongs to organizations that prioritize doing what is right over what is easy.

And in that future, whistleblowers are not villains—they are heroes.

Chapter 10: Common Ethical Dilemmas Across Industries

Ethical dilemmas are not abstract concepts—they are the everyday battles fought in boardrooms, hospitals, factories, and technology hubs worldwide. They often involve a painful trade-off between profits and principles, loyalty and law, convenience and conscience. No industry is immune.

Take Ellis Parker, a high-ranking investment banker at Sterling & Howdy, who was pressured to use insider information to make lucrative trades. Or Dr. Sarah Mehta a renowned oncologist at Clearwood Medical, who had to decide whether to approve an experimental but unproven drug for a desperate cancer patient.

These ethical dilemmas are real, messy, and difficult. They force professionals to question their integrity, often in situations where the wrong choice is easier than the right one.

This chapter explores five major industries and the most common ethical challenges they face, along with fictitious but realistic case studies of dilemmas and their resolutions.

Finance & Banking: Insider Trading, Bribery, and Fraud

The Pressure to Bend the Rules

Finance is a world driven by numbers, risks, and returns. But it is also a world where a small unethical decision can snowball into a massive scandal.

At Bravenscroft Securities, a top investment firm, Elias Park was known for his brilliant market instincts. One evening, over dinner with an old college friend—now a CFO of a pharmaceutical company—he casually learned that the company was about to announce a major breakthrough in Alzheimer's treatment.

The next morning, Elias had a choice.

Should he buy shares in the company before the public announcement? No one would know. It was a golden opportunity to make millions. Besides, he wasn't technically stealing the information—it was just a friendly conversation.

But deep down, he knew the truth. Acting on this knowledge would be insider trading, a crime that had ruined careers and destroyed reputations.

How the Dilemma Was Resolved

Instead of making the trade, Elias reported the situation to his company's compliance team. Though he lost a potential windfall, his decision protected his career and the integrity of his firm. The CFO friend, however, was later exposed for leaking confidential company information to other investors and faced prosecution.

Lesson: Ethical lapses in finance start small—a harmless tip, a small bribe, a "creative" accounting adjustment. But if left unchecked, they can destroy entire firms, as seen in real-world cases like Enron and Lehman Brothers.

Healthcare: Patient Privacy, Pharmaceutical Ethics, and Malpractice

The Cost of Doing the Right Thing

At Clearwood Medical Center, Dr. Sarah Mehta was in a moral quandary. A desperate father had approached her, begging her to approve a new experimental cancer drug for his dying daughter. The drug hadn't yet been FDA-approved, and early trials had mixed results.

If she approved it, she could give the girl a fighting chance—but also risk dangerous side effects. If she refused, the girl might die, and her family would never forgive her for not trying.

How the Dilemma Was Resolved

Dr. Mehta consulted her hospital's ethics board and legal team. She also spoke with the drug manufacturer for more trial data. In the end, she refused to approve the drug outside of a regulated clinical trial, but she worked with the family to get the patient into an expanded access program for experimental treatment.

The patient's condition did not improve, but Dr. Mehta's decision upheld medical ethics and protected future patients from unproven treatments.

Lesson: Healthcare ethics require balancing compassion with responsibility. Patients may beg for treatments that aren't ready, but medical professionals must prioritize science and safety.

Technology: Data Privacy, AI Ethics, and Misinformation

The Dark Side of AI Innovation

Oriental Technologies was a rising star in artificial intelligence. Their latest software, PersonifyAI, could analyze people's online activity and predict their personalities, spending habits, and even political views.

Lasoon Chea, a lead engineer, was thrilled about the potential—until she discovered that the AI was being used without user consent. The company's marketing team had quietly sold the data to political organizations, who were using it to manipulate voters through targeted disinformation campaigns.

Lasoon was horrified. This wasn't just about data privacy—it was about democracy itself.

How the Dilemma Was Resolved

Lasoon reported the issue to her company's ethics board, but leadership dismissed her concerns. Left with no other choice, she became a whistleblower, leaking the information to regulators and the press.

The scandal led to massive public backlash, lawsuits, and government intervention. Oriental Technologies suffered in the short term, but eventually rebuilt its reputation by committing to transparent AI policies.

Lesson: Technology companies must be guardians, not exploiters, of user data. Ethical tech professionals must push back against unethical practices, even at great personal risk.

Manufacturing & Retail: Labor Exploitation and Environmental Sustainability

The Hidden Cost of Cheap Goods

Evergreat Apparel was a global fashion brand known for trendy, affordable clothing. But when investigative journalists exposed that its factories in Bangladesh used child labor, CEO Mark Ramford faced a massive ethical dilemma.

Shutting down the factories would mean thousands of workers losing their jobs. But continuing operations meant turning a blind eye to exploitation.

How the Dilemma Was Resolved

Instead of denying the allegations, Mark acknowledged the issue and committed to change. Evergreat invested in third-party audits, ethical sourcing programs, and fair-wage initiatives.

Though this increased production costs, the company won back consumer trust and built a more sustainable, ethical supply chain.

Lesson: Ethical lapses in manufacturing are often hidden from consumers, but they can damage a brand overnight. Companies that proactively address labor rights and sustainability stand the test of time.

Human Resources: Bias in Hiring, Harassment, and Favoritism

When the Boss Protects a Predator

At NextBig Consulting, an ambitious young manager, Jaden Walter, was climbing the corporate ladder fast. But behind closed doors, he had a history of harassing female employees.

When HR director Angela Bakes received multiple complaints, she felt intense pressure from senior executives to dismiss the allegations. Jaden was a rising star, and leadership didn't want a scandal.

How the Dilemma Was Resolved

Instead of ignoring the complaints, Angela launched an independent investigation with legal oversight. The findings were undeniable. Despite the backlash, she recommended termination and overhauled the company's harassment policies.

The decision sent a strong message: No one—no matter how powerful—is above ethical accountability.

Lesson: HR professionals must have the courage to stand up to unethical leadership, even when it threatens their own career.

Final Thoughts: Doing the Right Thing in a Wrong World

Ethical dilemmas are never easy. The wrong choice is often faster, cheaper, and more convenient. But businesses built on ethical compromise eventually collapse under the weight of their own dishonesty. The professionals in these case studies made difficult choices at great personal cost, but their decisions created lasting change.

Every industry faces ethical crossroads. The question is:
When the moment comes, will you choose what is right—or what is easy?

SECTION 4:
RESOLVING ETHICAL CHALLENGES & IMPLEMENTING ACTION PLANS

Chapter 11: Strategies for Addressing & Resolving Ethical Challenges

Every organization, no matter how well-intentioned, will face ethical challenges. These are the defining moments that test the character of a company and its people. The way these challenges are addressed can determine whether an organization maintains its integrity or falls into a spiral of misconduct.

This chapter is about taking action. It's not just about identifying ethical problems—it's about solving them in a structured, transparent, and effective way. Ethical challenges don't resolve themselves. They require clear strategies, decisive leadership, and a culture where ethics is non-negotiable.

The Need for Ethical Decision-Making Playbooks

Imagine a pilot navigating a storm without a flight manual. That's what it's like for employees when they face ethical dilemmas without a clear decision-making playbook. In many cases, employees want to do the right thing, but they don't always know what the right thing is—or how to act without jeopardizing their careers.

Case Study: The Dilemma at Varden Pharmaceuticals

At Varden Pharmaceuticals, a scientist named Manny Mack discovered that a newly developed drug had severe side effects that were downplayed in internal reports. The drug was about to be launched, and billions of dollars were at stake. Manny knew that if he spoke up, he could risk his job and reputation. If he stayed silent, patients could suffer.

Without a structured decision-making process in place, Manny hesitated. He debated for weeks, growing increasingly anxious. His company had no ethical decision-making playbook, and he felt isolated.

In the end, he gathered the courage to report his findings directly to the FDA, but the delay caused irreversible damage to Varden's reputation. The company's leadership scrambled to control the fallout, and trust among employees was shattered.

How a Decision-Making Playbook Could Have Helped

A well-designed Ethical Decision-Making Playbook could have given Manny a structured path to report the issue internally before taking external action. It would have:

- ✓ Outlined step-by-step procedures for reporting ethical concerns.
- ✓ Specified protections for whistleblowers to ensure Mark felt safe.
- ✓ Provided clear accountability channels, ensuring leaders took immediate action.

Many companies fail to prevent ethical disasters not because they lack good people—but because they lack good systems. A playbook removes confusion, empowering employees to act with integrity without fear of retaliation.

Encouraging Open Communication & Ethical Reporting Systems

The most ethical organizations aren't the ones with zero reported problems. They're the ones where people feel safe enough to report issues without fear.

Why Employees Stay Silent

Many employees keep quiet about unethical behavior because they fear:

- ✓ Retaliation from managers or colleagues
- ✓ Being labeled as "troublemakers"
- ✓ Losing promotions or job security
- ✓ The belief that nothing will change

In the worst cases, a culture of silence allows minor ethical lapses to snowball into major corporate scandals.

Case Study: The Culture of Fear at Westway Bank

At Westway Bank, sales managers encouraged employees to open fake accounts without customer consent to meet aggressive sales targets. Junior employees saw this happening but didn't report it because:

- ✓ Their direct supervisors were involved.
- ✓ No anonymous reporting system existed.
- ✓ Whistleblowers in the past had been fired or ostracized.

By the time regulators discovered the fraud, the damage was done. The bank paid millions in fines, fired top executives, and lost public trust.

How Ethical Reporting Could Have Prevented the Scandal

If Westway Bank had built a strong ethical reporting system, employees would have had:

- ✓ A secure, anonymous hotline to report misconduct.
- ✓ Regular training on how to raise ethical concerns safely.
- ✓ A leadership team that encouraged open discussions about ethical concerns, rather than punishing employees for speaking up.

Action Plan for Building Ethical Reporting Systems:

- ✓ Create confidential reporting channels: Anonymous hotlines, third-party ombudsmen, and encrypted reporting platforms.
- ✓ Train employees regularly: Teach them how to report issues and protect themselves.
- ✓ Hold leaders accountable: No manager should be able to cover up misconduct.

Ethical reporting should be a sign of a healthy company, not a weakness. Employees must believe that reporting leads to positive action, not retaliation.

Developing Ethical Response Teams

Ethical challenges often escalate because no one is officially responsible for handling them. Many companies rely on HR or Legal to address issues, but these departments often lack specialized training in ethical crisis management.

An Ethical Response Team (ERT) is a dedicated group responsible for:

- ✓ Investigating ethical concerns
- ✓ Providing guidance to employees
- ✓ Recommending disciplinary action when necessary
- ✓ Building an Ethical Response Team

1. Appoint members from different departments – A mix of HR, Compliance, Operations, and Finance ensures a balanced approach.
2. Ensure independence – The team should report directly to the board, not company executives who might cover up problems.
3. Train the team in crisis management – They should be experts in ethical problem-solving and communication.

Case Study: How GrayCote Logistics Handled Bribery Allegations

At GrayCote Logistics, an employee discovered that a regional manager was paying bribes to government officials to secure contracts. The Ethical Response Team acted immediately, launching an internal investigation.

Instead of waiting for authorities to intervene, GrayCote:

- ✓ Self-reported the issue to regulators.
- ✓ Fired the involved employees and strengthened internal controls.
- ✓ Introduced strict anti-bribery training for all employees.

Because they took swift and transparent action, GrayCote avoided a larger scandal and even gained respect for their integrity.

Action Plans for Handling Ethical Crises

Even the best organizations will face ethical crises at some point. The key is not to avoid crises—but to handle them with integrity.

Step 1: Immediate Containment

When an ethical issue arises, stop the damage from spreading. If it's a financial scandal, freeze transactions. If it's a safety issue, pull the affected products immediately.

Step 2: Transparent Communication

Avoid the classic corporate mistake of hiding the truth. Cover-ups only make things worse. Be honest with employees, stakeholders, and the public.

Step 3: Independent Investigation

Internal teams may be biased. If the issue is serious, bring in third-party investigators to ensure fairness.

Step 4: Taking Corrective Action

Punishing only junior employees while protecting senior leaders destroys trust. Address systemic failures—not just individuals.

Step 5: Strengthening Policies for the Future

Every crisis is a learning opportunity. Once the issue is resolved, update policies, training, and safeguards to prevent it from happening again.

Final Thoughts: Courage & Action Over Silence

Ethical challenges don't disappear on their own. They demand action.

The organizations that thrive are those that:

- ✓ Empower employees to report concerns.
- ✓ Take ethical decision-making seriously.
- ✓ Respond to crises with transparency and accountability.

Ethics isn't just a set of rules. It's a culture, a mindset, and a commitment to doing the right thing—even when it's hard.

So the question isn't if your organization will face an ethical challenge. The real question is: ***Will you be prepared to handle it with integrity?***

Chapter 12:
Ethical Business Success Stories & Best Practices

Why Ethics and Success Go Hand in Hand

Many business leaders believe that success and ethics are at odds with each other—that to win in a competitive market, one must bend the rules. But history has proven otherwise. Ethical businesses don't just survive; they thrive. Customers trust them, employees stay loyal, and their long-term reputation attracts sustainable growth.

This chapter is about the companies that got it right—those that built strong ethical cultures, transformed from unethical beginnings, and demonstrated that integrity is not a weakness but a strength.

Case Study #1: Integrity Over Profits – The Rise of TrueTechno Solutions

The Ethical Stand That Changed an Industry

In the competitive world of technology consulting, TrueTechno Solutions was a rising star. Founded by Marlon West, a former engineer, the company gained a reputation for delivering cutting-edge software solutions to multinational corporations.

But TrueTechno faced its biggest ethical challenge when a billion-dollar client, Stanford Enterprises, requested something unusual. They wanted a backdoor feature in the software—a hidden function that would allow them to access user data without consent.

Marlon knew that complying would bring massive financial rewards. The contract alone was worth more than TrueTechno's annual revenue. Many of his investors and advisors urged him to agree, citing that "everyone does it" in the tech industry.

The Decision That Defined TrueTechno

Marlon refused. He believed in building technology that protected users, not exploited them. He walked away from the deal, knowing it could slow down his company's growth.

His decision caused a stir in the industry. Some called him naïve, while others admired his courage. But what happened next was unexpected—TrueTechno's ethical stance attracted attention from global regulators and advocacy groups.

Within months, the company secured new contracts from governments and ethical enterprises that valued data privacy. By standing firm on ethics, TrueTechno didn't just survive—it became an industry leader in cybersecurity solutions.

Key Lessons from TrueTechno's Success:

- ✓ Short-term sacrifices can lead to long-term gains. Ethics may seem costly initially, but they build trust and reputation.
- ✓ Customers value integrity. In an era of privacy concerns, users flock to companies they can trust.
- ✓ Employees rally behind ethical leadership. TrueTechno's workforce was proud to work for a company that stood for something bigger than profits.

Case Study #2: From Scandal to Redemption – The Transformation of Silver Crest Apparel

A Company on the Brink of Collapse

Silver Lining Apparel was once a beloved name in the fashion industry, known for its trendy yet affordable clothing. But behind the glamour was a web of unethical practices—the company outsourced production to factories with poor working conditions, child labor issues, and environmental violations.

When a journalist exposed these practices in a viral documentary, Silver Lining's reputation collapsed overnight. Major retailers dropped their products, protests erupted outside their stores, and the CEO, Brad Hoffman, was forced to resign.

With lawsuits piling up and customers boycotting their brand, the company had two options: shut down or rebuild.

A Radical Shift Towards Ethics

The newly appointed CEO, Dan Wayward, knew that half-measures wouldn't restore trust. He initiated a complete overhaul of Silver Lining's operations:

- ✓ He cut ties with unethical suppliers and partnered with fair-trade manufacturers.
- ✓ He introduced transparency reports, allowing customers to see where and how their clothes were made.
- ✓ He committed to environmentally friendly materials, even though they cost more.

The transition was painful and costly—profits dropped for two years as they rebuilt their supply chain. But slowly, the brand earned back public trust.

Today, Silver Lining is a case study in corporate redemption. Ethical fashion influencers support the brand, sales have surpassed pre-scandal levels, and their once-tainted reputation has turned into a symbol of change.

Key Lessons from Silver Lining's Transformation:

- ✓ Accountability is the first step to change. Acknowledging wrongdoing is necessary before progress can happen.
- ✓ Transparency rebuilds trust. Consumers are more forgiving when businesses show genuine efforts to improve.
- ✓ Long-term ethical investments pay off. Ethical operations might cost more initially but lead to brand loyalty and sustainable growth.

Best Practices from Ethical Organizations

The success of companies like TrueTechno and Silver Lining isn't accidental. Ethical businesses follow a set of best practices that ensure integrity becomes a part of their DNA.

1. Ethics is Not a Department—It's a Mindset

Many businesses treat ethics as something owned by HR or Compliance teams, but true ethical companies integrate ethics into every decision and department.

For example, at Sun Financial, a leading investment firm, employees don't just receive a one-time ethics training—they participate in quarterly discussions on ethical dilemmas in finance. This keeps ethics top-of-mind in everyday decision-making.

2. Leadership Must Set the Tone

If a company's leadership turns a blind eye to unethical behavior, it will spread through the organization. Ethical companies ensure that leaders set the right example.

Take Rhinestone Energy, a renewable energy firm. When a whistleblower reported potential misuse of government subsidies, CEO Sarah Martin did not cover it up or dismiss the complaint. Instead, she launched an internal audit, took corrective action, and publicly announced their commitment to ethical grant usage.

Her transparency strengthened the company's reputation, showing that ethics mattered at the top.

3. Reward Ethical Behavior, Not Just Performance

Many organizations reward performance at any cost, even if it encourages cutting corners. Ethical businesses, however, recognize and reward employees who make the right choices, even in tough situations.

At Evergreet Hospitality Group, an employee, Linda Massey, refused to accept bribes from a vendor promising "priority service" in exchange for an under-the-table payment. Instead of just thanking her, the company highlighted her ethical choice in a company-wide meeting, reinforcing that doing the right thing is valued just as much as hitting business targets.

Final Thoughts: Ethics is the Future of Business

The business world is full of companies that took shortcuts, made excuses, and ultimately collapsed under the weight of their own unethical practices. But the ones that last—the ones that build loyal customers, engaged employees, and strong reputations—are those that prioritize ethics, even when it's difficult.

What we learn from TrueTechno, Silver Lining, and other ethical businesses is this:

- ✓ Ethics is not just a compliance requirement; it's a competitive advantage.
- ✓ Ethical companies may struggle in the short term, but they win in the long run.
- ✓ Customers, employees, and investors are increasingly choosing businesses that stand for something bigger than profits.

So as you build your business, manage your team, or lead your organization, ask yourself: ***Are you making decisions today that will build an ethical legacy for tomorrow?***

Chapter 13: Implementing a Sustainable Ethical Culture

Why Ethics Must Be More Than Just a Policy

In today's fast-paced business world, companies often think of ethics as a set of rules—something to be printed in a handbook, mentioned in an onboarding session, and then largely forgotten. But true ethical culture isn't about policies—it's about behavior.

Companies that thrive ethically don't just talk about values; they embed them into every action, decision, and system within the organization. They ensure that ethics isn't just a requirement—it's a competitive advantage.

This chapter is about how to build an ethical culture that lasts, one that doesn't crumble under pressure, one that attracts the right people, and one that sustains the business for the long haul.

Making Ethics a Core Value and Business Advantage

When ethics is truly part of an organization's DNA, it does more than prevent wrongdoing—it creates opportunities. Ethical companies attract loyal customers, committed employees, and investors who believe in long-term value.

Consider Axis Consulting Group, a financial advisory firm that entered a highly competitive market in 2010. Most of their competitors made money by selling risky investment products that weren't always in the best interest of their clients.

Axis did the opposite. They built their reputation on radical transparency—clearly explaining risks to clients, refusing commissions from product vendors, and prioritizing long-term wealth creation over quick sales.

At first, growth was slow. Competitors outpaced them in revenue, and some industry leaders dismissed them as being "too idealistic". But over time, something incredible happened—clients began flocking to Axis because they trusted them.

By 2020, while many competitors faced lawsuits for misleading clients, Axis emerged stronger than ever, with a reputation that money couldn't buy.

The lesson? Ethics isn't just about avoiding scandals—it's a business strategy that builds trust, loyalty, and long-term success.

So, how can companies embed ethics as a true business advantage?

Hire for values, not just skills. Employees can learn technical skills, but integrity is non-negotiable. During hiring, Axis would ask candidates to describe a time they faced an ethical dilemma and how they handled it.

Incentivize ethical decisions. Axis rewarded employees who prioritized client interests over quick profits, ensuring that integrity wasn't just encouraged but actively reinforced.

Align ethics with business goals. Ethical culture must tie directly to profitability and strategy. Axis didn't just promote ethics; they demonstrated how transparency led to customer loyalty and stronger financial outcomes.

Ensuring Continuous Monitoring and Improvement

Building an ethical culture isn't a one-time initiative—it requires constant reinforcement and improvement. Just as companies track revenue, customer satisfaction, and productivity, they must also track ethical health.

Take the case of Higher Logistics, a growing supply chain company. In 2018, Higher's leadership assumed they had a strong ethical culture—after all, they had never had a major scandal.

But when they launched an internal ethics audit, they were shocked by what they found:

Some employees were being pressured to meet deadlines by ignoring safety protocols.

A few managers were accepting gifts from vendors in exchange for preferred contracts.

Lower-level employees feared speaking up about concerns because they didn't believe leadership would act.

These were warning signs of a culture that looked ethical on the surface but had growing cracks underneath.

Higher's leadership took immediate action:

- ✓ They launched an anonymous ethics hotline for employees to report concerns without fear.
- ✓ They changed performance metrics to include ethical compliance alongside financial goals.
- ✓ They introduced surprise audits to catch issues before they escalated into full-blown scandals.

Within two years, employee trust in leadership increased by 40%, ethical violations dropped significantly, and Higher's reputation in the industry improved dramatically.

The key takeaway? Ethics must be monitored like any other business function. Without oversight, even well-intentioned companies can slip into ethical blind spots.

Building Long-Term Mechanisms to Prevent Ethical Failures

History is full of businesses that once had strong reputations but collapsed due to ethical failures. The difference between companies that sustain integrity and those that crumble is whether they build long-term mechanisms to prevent failure.

Step 1: Establish an Independent Ethics Committee

Many companies rely on senior leadership to police ethics, but this is risky. Leaders can be biased, and conflicts of interest often arise.

A great example of long-term ethical governance comes from Evergreat Pharmaceuticals, a biotech firm specializing in life-saving medications. To ensure ethics remained a priority, Evergreat set up an independent Ethics Oversight Committee—a group of professionals outside of senior management tasked with reviewing corporate decisions, investigating ethical complaints, and enforcing accountability.

Step 2: Train Employees Continuously, Not Just Once

Ethical training is often treated as a one-time event during onboarding. But ethical dilemmas evolve, and training must evolve too.

At Astoria Foods, a global food supply company, ethics training isn't just a PowerPoint presentation during an employee's first week—it's a quarterly event that includes real-world case studies, role-playing exercises, and discussions about emerging challenges in the food industry.

Step 3: Implement Ethical Fail-Safes in Business Processes

Companies can't just rely on individuals to "do the right thing"—they must design processes that make unethical behavior difficult.

For instance, OrientRetail, a major e-commerce company, faced a growing issue of fake product reviews that manipulated customer purchasing decisions. Instead of relying solely on manual detection, they implemented an AI-driven review authentication system, eliminating fake reviews before they could mislead customers.

This proactive measure removed ethical temptations and ensured fairness in customer interactions.

Inspiring Future Leaders to Prioritize Ethics

Building a sustainable ethical culture requires more than rules and policies—it requires leaders who champion integrity at every level. The best way to secure an ethical future is to train and inspire the next generation of leaders to carry the torch.

Mentorship and Ethical Leadership Development

Ethical companies don't just focus on profits today—they invest in leaders for tomorrow. They ensure that mentorship programs and leadership training include ethics as a core focus.

At Standwell Consulting, a major strategy firm, future executives don't just learn about financial growth—they take part in Ethical Leadership Labs, where they analyze real ethical dilemmas faced by executives and debate the best courses of action.

Encouraging Courageous Decision-Making

One of the biggest barriers to ethical leadership is fear—fear of speaking up, fear of losing opportunities, fear of going against the majority.

That's why Beltic Media Group, a leading digital content company, runs an internal program called "The Ethics Challenge", where employees present real cases of ethical dilemmas they've faced (or could face) and discuss how they would handle them. The company rewards employees who show ethical courage, ensuring that integrity is seen as an asset, not a liability.

Final Thoughts: Ethics as a Legacy, Not a Trend

Ethical cultures don't just appear overnight—they are intentionally built, monitored, and reinforced.

Businesses that take ethics seriously don't just protect themselves from scandal—they create environments where employees thrive, customers trust, and profits grow sustainably.

The companies that last are the ones that ask themselves:

- ✓ Are we building a culture where ethics isn't optional, but essential?
- ✓ Are we continuously improving and monitoring our ethical health?
- ✓ Are we training future leaders to carry forward a legacy of integrity?

The answer to these questions determines whether a business survives for a few years—or leaves a lasting impact for generations.

Chapter 14: Action Plan Section Step-by-Step Guides to Implementing Ethical Practices

Building an ethical organization is not about having a polished value statement framed in the reception area. It's about the everyday decisions, conversations, and systems that shape the workplace. Ethical organizations aren't born—they are built through intentional action, steady leadership, and continuous reinforcement.

This chapter offers a comprehensive, step-by-step action plan for organizations and leaders who are serious about embedding ethics into their company culture. These steps are practical, implementable, and can be adapted across different industries and company sizes. The examples are entirely fictional but mirror real-world complexities to bring the content to life.

Step 1: Lay the Ethical Foundation

1.1 Define Core Ethical Values

Start by clearly articulating the ethical values your organization will stand for—truth, transparency, fairness, accountability, respect, and sustainability.

Example: *Vale Biotech*, a mid-sized pharmaceutical firm, began its transformation by rewording its core values. Instead of a vague "We act with integrity," they redefined it to:

"We commit to full scientific transparency, protect patient well-being above all else, and act as stewards of public trust."

Action Points:

- ✓ Involve cross-functional teams in value discussions.
- ✓ Translate each value into clear behaviors and examples.
- ✓ Display these in every department and communication channel.

Step 2: Build the Framework – Governance & Policy

2.1 Develop a Practical Code of Ethics

Avoid dense legal jargon. Make your code readable, visual, and scenario-based.

Example: *Orient Logistics* created an "Ethics Playbook" with short, comic-strip-style scenarios on bribery, confidentiality, and conflict of interest. It became one of their most downloaded internal documents.

Action Points:

- ✓ Include real-life dilemmas employees face.
- ✓ Provide a "What to do when…" section in each area.
- ✓ Translate the code into local languages if operating globally.

2.2 Set Up Ethics Governance

Create an Ethics Committee or Officer to own this process. They should report directly to the board or CEO for true independence.

Checklist:

- ✓ Ethics Officer appointed?
- ✓ Regular ethics risk assessments scheduled?
- ✓ Whistleblower protection policies in place?
- ✓ Anonymous reporting channels established?

Step 3: Embed Ethics in Hiring, Onboarding & Training

3.1 Integrate Ethics into Hiring

Ensure interviews assess ethical thinking, not just skillsets.

Example: *AllBig Retail* includes scenario-based questions like: "If a top vendor offers you a gift worth ₹50,000 to push a purchase order urgently, what would you do?"

They assess not only the answer, but the reasoning behind it.

Action Points:

- ✓ Train recruiters and managers to identify ethical reasoning.
- ✓ Add ethics-related scenarios to every job simulation or test.
- ✓ Ensure clarity in job descriptions about the ethical culture.

3.2 Ethical Onboarding

New employees form habits early. Begin with a strong ethical orientation.

Best Practices:

- ✓ Conduct an "Ethics First" onboarding session led by top leaders.
- ✓ Walk them through real stories—both failures and victories.
- ✓ Assign an "Ethics Buddy" for the first 3 months.

Step 4: Make Ethics Operational – Integrate in Daily Workflows

4.1 Department-Level Ethics Protocols

Every team—from finance to frontline sales—should customize ethics protocols relevant to their tasks.

Example: *V-Energy's* field teams in remote areas had a simple rule: Never pay facilitation fees to local agents. Instead, they built a "Community Engagement Handbook" outlining alternative legal ways to build goodwill without bribes.

Action Points:

- ✓ Conduct "ethical risk mapping" by department.
- ✓ Draft do's and don'ts guides tailored to common challenges.
- ✓ Involve frontline employees in designing practical guides.

4.2 Decision-Making Checklists

Incorporate ethics into standard decision-making checklists and approval workflows.

Mini Checklist Sample: Before approving a vendor contract:

- ✓ Was the selection process transparent and documented?
- ✓ Are there any known personal connections?
- ✓ Does this vendor align with our social/environmental values?

Step 5: Leadership Alignment & Role Modeling

5.1 Train Leaders to be Ethical Role Models

Ethics trickles down from the top. Without visible, consistent role modeling, the rest is noise.

Example: At *Gavin Insurance*, the CEO regularly shares "Moments of Integrity" emails spotlighting employees who made difficult but ethical choices. One team member declined a lucrative client due to suspected money laundering. She was publicly celebrated and given a bonus.

Action Points:

- ✓ Run regular ethical leadership workshops.

- ✓ Encourage transparency in executive decisions.
- ✓ Recognize and reward ethical behavior at leadership levels.

Step 6: Encourage Reporting & Protect Whistleblowers

6.1 Set Up Multiple Reporting Channels

Options must include in-person, email, helpline, and anonymous online forms.

6.2 Build Trust in the System Employees must believe they won't be punished for reporting.

Example: *Joseph Engineering* instituted a "No Retaliation Guarantee." Over time, reports went up—but violations decreased. People started correcting one another earlier because there was cultural permission to speak up.

Action Points:

- ✓ Assign a neutral department (e.g., Ethics or Ombudsman) to manage reports.
- ✓ Publish sanitized reports of resolved issues in internal newsletters.
- ✓ Track retaliation complaints aggressively.

Step 7: Monitor, Measure & Improve Continuously

7.1 Conduct Regular Ethics Audits

Track key indicators: complaint frequency, investigation speed, department-wise risk, employee trust surveys.

Checklist for Quarterly Ethics Review:

- ✓ Number and resolution rate of ethics complaints
- ✓ Training completion rates
- ✓ High-risk departments and recurring themes

- ✓ Cultural pulse via internal surveys

7.2 Annual Ethics Maturity Score

Create an annual "Ethics Report Card" to track organizational growth.

Sample Scorecard Indicators:

Area	Score (1-5)	Notes
Leadership Role Modeling	4	Visible, but needs more storytelling
Ethics Training Completion	5	100% of workforce trained
Whistleblower Trust	3	Hotline exists but needs awareness
Transparency in Operations	4	Procurement reports published quarterly

Step 8: Celebrate & Sustain the Ethical Culture

Celebrate not just success, but the way success is achieved.

Example: Each year, *MoCare Hospitals* hosts an "Ethical Champions Gala" honoring staff who upheld ethics in difficult situations. Winning stories are dramatized in company videos and induction training.

Ideas to Sustain Culture:

- ✓ Create short films based on real ethical dilemmas resolved well.
- ✓ Offer "Integrity Awards" at annual functions.
- ✓ Include an ethics metric in performance appraisals.

Final Thought: Ethics Is Not an Add-On—It *Is* the Business

Ethics isn't a department, a manual, or a compliance burden. It is the *soul of the organization*. Implementing ethical practices is not about ticking boxes—it's about creating a workplace where people feel proud, safe, and inspired. The steps in this action plan are not final. They are the beginning of a culture that must be nurtured continuously, courageously, and collectively.

Chapter 15:
Ethical Decision-Making Toolkits: Practical Templates, Checklists, and Self-Assessment Tools

In the fast-paced and high-pressure environment of the corporate world, ethics often finds itself wrestling with profit, politics, and personal ambition. Most professionals do not wake up intending to make unethical decisions. They are often caught in gray zones, pressured by deadlines, incentives, or cultural norms that subtly reward compromise. This is where practical tools come into play—tools that bring clarity, structure, and a sense of direction to ethical decision-making.

This chapter presents a set of simple, powerful toolkits to help individuals and organizations strengthen their ethical compass. Whether you're a team lead, manager, or CEO, these tools can be integrated into everyday workflows and decision-making processes to promote integrity, trust, and accountability.

---

1. The E.D.G.E. Framework – A 4-Step Ethical Decision Guide

E.D.G.E. stands for:

- ✓ Evaluate the Situation
- ✓ Determine the Stakeholders
- ✓ Guide the Decision with Principles
- ✓ Execute with Accountability

Use Case Example: Anna, a procurement officer at *Torrent Manufacturing*, receives an offer from a vendor for a luxury trip in exchange for awarding a

contract. She feels uncertain, especially since senior managers often look the other way.
Let's apply the E.D.G.E. Framework:
Evaluate the Situation:

- ✓ Is this a gift or a bribe?
- ✓ Does this violate company policy or industry standards?

Determine the Stakeholders:

- ✓ Customers who expect ethical sourcing
- ✓ The procurement team's reputation
- ✓ Competing vendors treated unfairly

Guide with Principles:

- ✓ Torrent's Code of Conduct prohibits gifts of high value
- ✓ Integrity and transparency are core organizational values

Execute with Accountability:

- ✓ Anna politely declines the offer in writing and documents the incident
- ✓ She reports it to her supervisor and compliance team

Toolkit Template:

Step	Key Questions	Your Input
Evaluate	What is the core issue? Is it legal? Is it transparent?	
Determine	Who is impacted? Who could be harmed or benefit?	
Guide	What values or policies apply? What does your conscience say?	
Execute	What action will you take? Who needs to be informed?	

2. Personal Ethics Self-Assessment Checklist

This tool helps individuals evaluate how ethically aligned their decisions and actions are in their current role.

Instructions: Mark each statement as **Always**, **Sometimes**, or **Never**

Statement	Always	Sometimes	Never
I consider the impact of my decisions on all stakeholders			
I avoid actions that would embarrass me if they were made public			
I speak up when I see something wrong, even if it's uncomfortable			
I understand my organization's ethical policies and abide by them			
I avoid conflicts of interest and disclose them when they arise			
I hold myself accountable for both outcomes and the means of achieving them			

Interpretation:

Mostly Always: You're aligned with strong ethical behavior.

Mix of Sometimes/Never: Reflect on what's holding you back and develop an action plan.

3. Ethical Risk Assessment Grid

This tool helps managers assess which functions or departments may be vulnerable to ethical breaches.

Use Case Example: Graffings Fintech wants to ensure its new customer onboarding process is compliant and transparent.

Assessment Grid:

Department/Process	Risk Level (Low/Medium/High)	Ethical Concern	Action Required
Customer Onboarding	High	Misuse of personal data	Introduce stricter data policies
Sales Incentive Plan	Medium	Overpromising products	Revise targets & training
Vendor Selection	High	Kickbacks or favoritism	Rotate decision panels

This grid allows leadership to pre-emptively tackle issues before they become crises.

4. The Whistleblower Pathway Flowchart

One of the most powerful signs of an ethical organization is how safe and clear it makes whistleblowing. This tool provides a clear decision path for employees wondering whether—and how—to report something unethical.

Example:

START

↓

Have you witnessed a policy or legal violation?

→ Yes

↓

Can you discuss it with your direct manager safely?

→ No

↓

Use the anonymous reporting hotline or escalate to the Ethics Committee

↓

Document everything and seek support

↓

You are protected by company policy and whistleblower rights

Make this flowchart available on your company's intranet or orientation documents. Employees must feel that the pathway is real—not performative.

5. Ethics Meeting Template for Team Reviews

Embed ethics into the rhythm of the business. Here's a simple meeting template that can be used quarterly or during retrospectives.

Team Ethics Review Agenda Template:

Topic	Notes/Discussion	Action Plan
Ethical concerns raised last quarter	Were there any? What patterns are emerging?	Investigate/report/revise
Policy clarity	Are there gray areas?	Create FAQs, provide training
Role-model behaviors observed	Who demonstrated outstanding integrity?	Recognize and share examples
Team pressures	Are any internal KPIs causing ethical shortcuts?	Adjust KPIs or timelines

6. Quick 5-Minute "Gut Check" Tool

Sometimes decisions come fast. Here's a powerful mini-tool that helps in high-pressure moments.

Ask Yourself:

- ✓ Would I be comfortable explaining this decision to my children?
- ✓ Would I be okay if this was on the front page of the newspaper?
- ✓ Does this decision reflect the best version of myself and this company?
- ✓ Would this action still be right if everyone else did the same?
- ✓ Is this a short-term win at the cost of long-term trust?

If you answer NO or feel uneasy about any of these, pause, seek counsel, and reconsider.

Final Action Plan: Building Toolkit Habits

- ✓ Customize the templates shared in this chapter to fit your company's culture.
- ✓ Use the Ethics Grid during strategic reviews and risk assessments every six months.
- ✓ Create a dedicated "Ethics Folder" for every team on your shared drive. Include all tools from this chapter.
- ✓ Train leaders and line managers on using these templates during team meetings and performance reviews.
- ✓ Encourage anonymous feedback on these tools—make it clear they are dynamic and evolving.
- ✓ Reward tool usage. If someone uses a toolkit to resolve an issue, share the story (while protecting anonymity, if needed).

Closing Reflection

Ethics isn't a theoretical luxury. It's a practical skill, a system of habits, and a set of muscles you train like any other. These toolkits are not meant to make you a moral perfectionist—they are here to help you be intentional, accountable, and courageous. A culture of ethics is built one decision at a time, and these tools are your scaffolding for that journey.

Conclusion & Final Thoughts

The Power of Ethical Decision-Making in Transforming Businesses

Ethics is not a luxury. It is not something that businesses can afford to consider only when convenient. It is the foundation upon which trust is built, reputations are strengthened, and long-term success is secured.

Time and time again, we have seen companies rise and fall based not on their products, services, or strategies but on the ethical choices they make every day. Some businesses have gone from small startups to global giants because they built trust through ethical decision-making. Others have collapsed despite financial success because they ignored ethics and paid the price.

Take the example of Northway Technologies, a once-prominent software firm that pioneered groundbreaking AI tools. When artificial intelligence began shaping multiple industries, Northway had the first-mover advantage. Investors were eager to pour in money, and clients were lining up to use their products.

But behind the scenes, unethical practices were eating away at their foundation. Their leadership ignored privacy concerns, allowed biased algorithms to manipulate search results, and secretly sold user data to third parties. For a while, the profits were astronomical.

Then, the inevitable happened. A whistleblower within the company exposed their practices, triggering a massive scandal. Lawsuits followed. Clients abandoned them. Regulatory authorities imposed crippling fines. In just two years, Northway Technologies went from a leader in innovation to a case study in corporate self-destruction.

Now, contrast this with Orient Healthcare, a pharmaceutical company that faced an ethical dilemma when a competitor rushed a new drug to market without completing proper safety trials. Orient's investors pressured them to do the same to avoid falling behind. But Orient's leadership made a tough decision—they refused to cut corners, even if it meant delaying their product launch.

At first, the decision seemed like a financial mistake. The competitor's drug hit the shelves first, and their stock soared. However, within months, reports surfaced that the drug had severe side effects, leading to hospitalizations and recalls. In the end, Orient Healthcare's ethical stance saved lives, preserved their reputation, and secured their position as an industry leader for years to come.

The lesson is clear: Ethics may not always provide instant rewards, but in the long run, it determines who survives and who collapses.

Why Ethical Organizations Thrive in the Long Run

The world is changing. Consumers, employees, and investors are no longer satisfied with businesses that only focus on profits. They demand companies that operate with integrity, transparency, and accountability.

Studies have consistently shown that companies with strong ethical cultures outperform their competitors in the long run. Ethical organizations attract:

- ✓ Loyal customers who trust their brand

- ✓ Dedicated employees who feel valued and respected
- ✓ Investors who seek long-term sustainability, not just short-term gains

Consider the story of Everbright Retail, a chain of eco-friendly stores that started in a small town. While competitors maximized profits by using cheap, unsustainable materials and exploiting low-wage labor, Everbright took the harder path. They committed to fair wages, ethical sourcing, and environmentally responsible practices.

For years, they struggled to keep up with the industry giants. But as consumer preferences shifted toward ethical shopping, Everbright's commitment paid off. Customers became loyal advocates, their workforce was highly engaged, and they expanded from a local shop to an international brand.

In contrast, several of their competitors who chased short-term profits through unethical means faced public backlash, lawsuits, and declining sales.

The success of businesses like Everbright proves that ethics isn't just a moral obligation—it's a business strategy for long-term resilience and growth.

But this isn't just about companies. Ethics is shaped by individuals at every level. It is not just the responsibility of CEOs or compliance teams. It starts with the everyday choices of employees, managers, and leaders.

How Individuals at All Levels Can Become Ethics Champions

Every person in an organization has the power to influence its ethical culture. It doesn't require a high-ranking position—it requires courage, consistency, and a commitment to doing what's right, even when it's difficult.

Think about Daniel Carter, a mid-level accountant at a multinational firm. One day, he discovered irregularities in financial reports that pointed to fraud at the senior management level. He faced a dilemma: stay silent and protect his career, or speak up and risk everything.

Despite the risks, Daniel chose to report his findings through the company's ethics hotline. His courage led to a full-scale internal investigation, exposing a scandal that could have destroyed the company if left unchecked. Instead of being punished, Daniel was later promoted for his integrity and leadership in protecting the company's reputation.

Daniel wasn't a CEO. He wasn't a compliance officer. He was just one employee who refused to look the other way.

Anyone can be an ethics champion in their own way:

- ✓ A sales executive who refuses to lie to customers just to meet a quota.
- ✓ A manager who ensures fair promotions instead of playing favorites.
- ✓ A team leader who creates a safe space for employees to voice concerns.

Ethical leadership doesn't always make headlines, but it is the silent force that shapes a company's destiny.

For those who wonder whether one person's ethical choices can really make a difference, the answer is simple: **yes.**

Because when one person stands for integrity, it creates a ripple effect. Others take notice. Ethical behavior becomes the norm. An organization transforms.

Final Reflections: Ethics is Not a Burden—It is a Legacy

Ethics is often seen as a challenge—something that requires sacrifice, discipline, and difficult decisions. But in reality, ethics is a legacy. It is what separates businesses that make a quick profit from those that change the world.

Every organization, every leader, every employee must ask themselves:

- ✓ Are we building a culture that values ethics, or are we simply avoiding legal trouble?
- ✓ Are we willing to prioritize integrity, even when it's inconvenient?
- ✓ Are we setting an example that future generations will be proud of?

The companies and individuals that answer yes to these questions are the ones that will stand the test of time.

In the end, ethics is not just about avoiding wrongdoing—it is about doing what is right, every single day, at every level, in every decision.

And when enough people and businesses commit to that path, they don't just succeed—they inspire a world where trust, fairness, and integrity define the way we do business.

About the Author 'GERARD ASSEY'

Gerard Assey is a Graduate in Economics, a PGD in Management (HRD) and holds a Doctorate in Leadership. Gerard holds several International Qualifications in Sales, Debt Collection, Training & Teaching, and is a 'Fellow' of the prestigious 'Institute of Sales & Marketing Management'-UK, a Certified NLP Practitioner, a 'Certified Trainer', an 'Accredited Management Teacher-Behavioral Sciences', a 'Certified Competency Facilitator', a 'Certified Management Consultant'- (the International credentials of a professional management consultant, awarded in accordance with global standards of the ICMCI); and a Certification from the University of Michigan in 'Successful Negotiation: Essential Strategies and Skills'

He is also a Member of the 'National Association of Sales Professionals' backed with several years experience in varied industries, both in India and Overseas. He also holds an 'Etiquette Consultant' Certification from the USA (by Sue Fox, Author of Best Seller: 'Business Etiquette for Dummies'. She has trained some of the top celebrities' world over). He was also a recipient of a scholarship for extensive training in Japan on 'Corporate Management for India'.

Gerard Assey is 'Founder & Chief Corporate Trainer' of the Group: '**Citius, Altius, Fortius Unlimited'**- an organization that **celebrated 20 years of Glorious Service** in 2021, focusing on 3 Core Competencies:

People. Performance. Profit; in functional areas of Sales & Marketing, HR & Organizational Development, covering Recruitment, Training & Consultancy!

Having managed organizations with large Sales Forces in India & Overseas, his specialization cover extensive areas of Sales Training (All levels - Presentation, Negotiation, Key/ Strategic Accounts Management & Managerial Skills for all sectors), Bid Proposal/ Capture Planning/ Management Trainings, Retail Sales, Customer Service & Customer Retention Programs, Training for Prevention & Collection of Debt, Self & Personal Development Programs (Time Management, Teamwork & Team Building, Business Etiquette & Personal Grooming, Leadership & Managerial Skills, People Management Skills, Train-the-Trainer etc), including preparation of Custom-designed Business Manuals for Internal (HR, Induction, and Sales etc) & External use (Instruction, User Manuals).

Gerard has successfully conducted over 6450 Trainings & Workshops (as of April '25) all across India, Middle East, Africa, Europe & S.E. Asia. Besides public programs conducted regularly, both in India & Overseas, he has some of the top names as clients whom he services from Single Owners to large Public & Government undertakings, covering all sectors, for their in-house needs.

His website: www.CollectionSkills.com is the only one in this part of the world to be featured in the 'Collections & Credit Risk Magazine-USA' under 'Who's Who in Training' and ranks TOP, along with other websites listed below on most search engines.

Gerard is author of 189 books already (April 2025), all the books being available on all online platforms and outlets as E-books and Paperbacks

A few of our business related books:

1. Bite-sized Bits on Commonsense Management
2. Heart to Heart on Life's Principles'
3. How to become a Successful Manager
4. The Sales Professionals' Master Workbook of S.Y.S.T.E.M.S
5. The Professional Business Email Etiquette Handbook & Guide
6. The Professional Business Video-Conferencing Etiquette Handbook & Guide
7. Professional Presentation Skills
8. Exceptional Customer Service
9. Professional Tele-Marketing Skills
10. Professional Debt Collection Skills
11. The G.R.E.A.T. Sales & Service Workbook
12. Sales Training Advantage for Results (*The Ultimate Sales Training Manual to enable you stand out as a S.T.A.R.*)
13. CEO Daily Planner & Organizer
14. The Sales Professionals' Master Daily Planner
15. The Professional Debt Collector's Master Daily Planner
16. My Daily Planner & Organizer
17. MY EMERGENCY INFORMATION RECORD (Family Emergency & Peace of Mind Planner)
18. The Ultimate Therapist & Counselors Planner and Organizer
19. Building an Ethical Workplace
20. Managing Relationships at Work
21. Managing Business Meetings Effectively
22. Effective Delegation Skills
23. Goal Setting for Success
24. B2B Selling by Email
25. Professional Business Etiquette & Grooming
26. Dining Etiquette & Table Manners
27. Effective Networking Skills
28. Grooming, Etiquette & Manners for Teens, Young Adults & Future Leaders
29. Inter-Personal Skills
30. Get Ready, Get Hired!
31. Selling in a Recession
32. Effective Receivables Management in an Economic Downturn!
33. Real Estate & Property Sales Training
34. Credit Sales & Accounts Receivable Management

35. Selling Skills for Real Estate & Property Advisors
36. Take G.R.E.A.T. C.A.R.E!
37. Spa, Salon & Health Club Selling Skills
38. Selling Travel, Holiday & MICE Services
39. Selling Skills for Spa's, Salons & Health Clubs
40. Retailing in Salons & Spas
41. Selling Holiday, Vacation, Tours & Packages
42. The Power of Sales Referrals
43. Selling Luxury
44. Technical Selling Skills
45. Financial Advisors Sales Training
46. Dealing with Burnout at Work Monopolize Your Markets
47. Selling to Affluent Customers
48. Growing up with Grace
49. Financial Selling Skills
50. *The Effective Manager's Guide: Key Skills to Thrive*
51. From Aspiring to Inspiring: A Guide for New Managers on the Rise
52. The Power of Focus
53. Selling with Integrity: Sell Like Jesus The Perfect Role Model!
54. 31 Habits of Champions: Your 31-Day Journey to Greatness
55. Rejecting Grasshopper Talk: From Grasshopper to Giant-Killer-*Defeating Giants Daily!*
56. Navigate the AI-Powered Future of Bid & Proposals: Up-Skill to Stay Relevant with Alternative Career Paths & Opportunities
57. Hiring Sales Winners
58. Present with Impact
59. Success Unlocked: *Breaking Free from Habits that Hold You Back*
60. Complaints to Cheers, Feedback to Gold: Mastering Complaints Management
61. Thriving Together: *Cultivating Diversity, Equity, and Inclusion*
62. Coaching Skills for Sales Managers
63. Soaring to Success in Business & Leadership: Swifter, Higher, Stronger!
64. From Classroom to Podium: A Student's Guide to Powerful Public Speaking & Presentation Skills
65. Developing Self-Discipline
66. The CEO's 31-Day Power Plan: Unlocking Success through Essential Traits

67. Credibility Matters
68. A Winning Attitude
69. Bid & Proposal Management Using AI
70. Sales Forecasting: A Practical & Proven Guide to Strategic Sales Forecasting
71. Elevate & Energize: *50 Dynamic & Fun Activities for Peak Workplace Morale*
72. 'Sales SOS! Sales on Fire! *30 Days to Conquer Chaos & the Nightmares of Success!'*
73. Mastering Sales Managerial Skills: *Building High-Performing Teams & Driving Exceptional Results*
74. Eagle-Eyed Leadership: Unleashing the Power of 31 Lessons from Eagles
75. The Ultimate Employee Training Guide: *Training Today, Leading Tomorrow*
76. Being More Accountable at Work
77. Creating a Culture of Continuous Improvement
78. Effective Questioning & Listening Skills
79. The Power of Value Selling
80. The Growth Mindset
81. Mastering Professional Help Desk Skills
82. The Power to Lead with Empathy
83. Being Prepared: The Key to Unlocking Success
84. Youthful Spark-Youth Energizers, Activities and Games-Igniting the Fun in Youth
85. Ignite your Motivation for Success
86. Elevate Your Executive Presence: *Your Roadmap to Executive Excellence*
87. Smart Decisions: *Mastering Problem Solving with Strategic Solutions for Business Success*
88. Strategic Planning: *Developing and Implementing Strategic Plans to Achieve Long-Term Business Goals*
89. The Power of Stay Interviews
90. Developing G.R.I.T.
91. Adaptability
92. Diagnosis- *A Key Skill for Leadership*
93. The Burnout-Proof Salesperson: *The Master Guide to Preventing Stress & Burnout-* Strategies for Thriving in Sales
94. Learning from Failure: *Keys to Success*
95. Customer Success Management
96. Overcoming the Killers of Motivation
97. The C-Suite Code: *Mastering Skills for Executive Excellence'*

98. Dealing with Difficult Customers
99. Unlocking Your Potential: Mastering the Top 20 Life Skills for a Brighter Future
100. Nurturing Tomorrow's Leaders: *Essential Soft Skills Every Child Must Learn*
101. Lively & Fun Party Games for Seniors & Elders
102. Role Playing for Sales Champions: From Practice to Performance
103. Fun and Exciting Party Games for Kids
104. Case Studies for Sales
105. Role-Playing for Unbeatable Customer Service
106. Case Studies in Customer Service
107. Case Studies in Winning Negotiations
108. Case Studies in Management & Leadership
109. Case Studies in Human Resources & Talent Management
110. CEO Success Blueprint: The Essential Toolkit for CEOs and C-Level Executives
111. The Salesperson's Self-Coaching Guide: *Master Your Own Self-Coaching Plan for Success*
112. Overcoming Procrastination: *Your Ultimate Guide to Stop Delaying and Start Living Your Best Life*
113. When True Colors Are Exposed: *The Journey to Unmasking Humanity*
114. Life-Changing Habits for Teens: Teen Success Blueprint for a Bright Future
115. Workplace Stress-Free: *Proven Strategies to Thrive at Work and Beyond*
116. Objection Overruled: *The Ultimate Guide to Turning 'No' into 'Yes'"*
117. Building Strong Teams: *A Comprehensive Guide to Team Building*
118. Ethical & Moral Leadership in Business: *Eliminating Unethical Practices & Building a Culture of Trust & Integrity*

Besides regularly contributing to business & trade journals, including international ones such as the 'Creative Training Techniques' and the 'Sales News' of the U.S.A, He is also a member of several prestigious bodies & trade associations, having participated in many Conferences & Workshops in India & Overseas.

Prior to his last assignment of leading & managing a large MNC as head, Gerard had a 3-year stint in the Middle East as a Consultant with a leading British Consultancy Firm.

As the past 'Official Country Representative' for the International Business Award- 'THE STEVIES'-(the business world's own Oscar) for about 4 years- he ensured a few Indian companies that qualify for the same every year!

Gerard can be contacted at:
Email: training@Sales-Training.in,training@CollectionSkills.com
Websites:

www.Sales-Training.in
www.EtiquetteWorks.in
www.CollectionSkills.com
www.RetailSalesTraining.in
www.SalesTrainingIndia.com
www.ManualPreparation.com
www.TrainingWithPuppets.com
www.FirstContactAcademy.com
www.SalesAndMarketingRecruiter.com

Our TRAININGS that can help your team

- ✓ **Sales Effectiveness**: Selling Skills for any Sector: Service/ Logistics/ FMCG Realty/ Insurance & Finance/ Media/ SPA's, Health Clubs & Salons/ Key Account Management, Effective Negotiation Skills/ Bid & Proposal Management Skills/ Retail Sales Training: Any Sector (Auto, Jewelry, Clothing, Luxury etc)
- ✓ **Customer Service Skills**-Complaints Handling & Customer Retention
- ✓ **Debt Prevention & Collection Skills**
- ✓ **Etiquette & Grooming**
- ✓ **Leadership & Managerial Skills**
- ✓ **Self & Personal Development Skills**: Presentation Skills/ Effective Communication Skills/Business Proposal Writing Skills/ Problem Solving & Decision Making Skills/ Empowering Secretaries-The perfect PA! (For Secretaries & PA's)/ Effective Time Management/ Teamwork & Teambuilding/ P.R.I.D.E- **P**ersonal **R**esponsibility **I**n **D**elivering **E**xcellence

www.ingramcontent.com/pod-product-compliance
Ingram Content Group UK Ltd.
Pitfield, Milton Keynes, MK11 3LW, UK
UKHW021340190726
13845UKWH00027B/649

9 788198 569189